RURAL POVERTY

RURAL POVERTY

(An Analytical Study)

By

Ram Sakal Singh

ANMOL PUBLICATIONS PVT. LTD.

NEW DELHI - 110 002 (INDIA)

ANMOL PUBLICATIONS PVT. LTD.
H.O.: 4374/4B, Ansari Road, Daryaganj
New Delhi - 110 002
Ph.: 23261597, 23278000
B.O.: No. 1015, Ist Main Road, BSK III Stage
III Phase, III Block
Bangalore - 560 085 (India)
Visit us at: www.anmolpublications.com

Rural Poverty: An Analytical Study

First Published, 2006

ISBN 81-261-2640-X

PRINTED IN INDIA

Published by J.L. Kumar for Anmol Publications Pvt. Ltd., New Delhi - 110 002 and Printed at Mehra Offset Press, Delhi.

Contents

Contents

Acknowledgements

One of the greatest problems before the Government of India has been to alleviate poverty from the country and improve socio-economic status of the poor and deprived sections of the people. Socio-economic justice is a global term. This demanded a basic change in the economic policy and administrative framework. The administration pattern established by the British Government did not touch welfare scheme. The framers of the Indian Constitution were fully aware of this fact. That is why they encorporated certain principles of socialistic pattern of society. But the constitution did not provide a suitable administrative pattern to give effect to the economic policies. The Government of Mrs. Indira Gandhi took decisive step in this regard. Before her, there was Community Development Project with the responsibility to change the rural face of India. Later, on the basis of the recommendations of the Ashok Mehta Committee the Village Panchayat System was brought into effect. To enable the rural people to participate in economic development and grassroot level problems, power were decentralised. Development Blocks and incubments associated with the Block Development were empowered to work for Rural Development, but not much ice was cut. Mrs. Indira Gandhi's Government adopted some centrally sponsored schemes which were supported and extented by her successors. These schemes mostly run under I.R.D.P., N.R.E.G.P., J.R.Y. etc. are running all over the nation Many officials and Government workers are actively engaged in implementing these schemes. Implementations of these schemes and projects need close verification and analysis.

The U.G.C. has proposed various types of study under Rural

Development Programmes and administrative change. I have adopted one of such projects under the inspiration of U.G.C.

Since the work is under the scheme of U.G.C. and U.G.C. is the financer of the project, I express my obligation to it for offering me to complete this project.

The First Chapter of this work gives a detailed description of the people and their economic conditions before and after arrival the British in India.

The Second Chapter studies the Objectives of the Community Development Plan and critically analyses the achievement and failures of the Community Development Plan.

The Third Chapter presents a detailed study of the Policies of the Government with regard to Rural Development.

Chapter Fourth, namely, Integrated Rural Development Programmes The Government initiated a countrywide popular programme known as the I.R.D.P. with the objectives to remove mass poverty from the rural field.

Chapter Fifth, discussed and examines the Objectives and Effectiveness of these Programmes.

Chapter Sixth, studies objectively and examines deeply the objectives of J.R.Y. and its implementation.

The last Chapter, presents Recent Special Schemes and Agencies for Development of Rural Poor and presents a short descriptive and critical account of the recent steps of the Government of India in the field of eradication of poverty from the rural field.

First and foremost I am and will always remain, under the deepest debt of gratitude to Dr. Kamaldeo Narayan Singh, Principal, Nalanda College, Biharsharif, Nalanda without whose loving and sincere care, this research project never could be completed.

I am thankful to Joint Secretary, University Grants Commission, Eastern Regional Office, Kolkata, for financial assistance for undertaking Minor Research Project to No. F.P.H.B. - 7/90 (ERO) dated August 99-2000.

Dr. Ram Sakal Singh

Introduction

Despite tremendous industrial growth in the country, India is virtually rural in its spirit and structure. Majority of the Indians are rural inhabitants whose economic condition is yet vulernable. Nearly fifty per cent of the people are still below the line of poverty. There are millions of Indians who are half-clothed and half-fed. They have no home to live. They are victims of starvation. They easily fell victims to various diseases due to lack of proper sanitation and medical facilities. It is a mockery to note that India is rich in its economic resources, but its most of the people are still living in acute scarcity of essential needs of the life. The government got the problem of economic backwardness of the country as a legacy of the British rule in India. The British rule in India for nearly two centuries, but did little to improve the economic condition of the people who lived in rural areas. A general study of the British economic policies in India reveals the fact that their basic aim was to exploit Indian economic resources for gaining maximum profits at the cost of the poor. The British pattern of administration in India was best inclined towards general welfare of the people. Rather it stood to exploit the people. When India achieved Independence, poverty in the country had crossed the limit. The people specially in the rural India, except a few landlords and Zamindars, were drawn into the ocean of miseries, troubles and scarcity. The government of democratic India had to start with a new begging to fight with such Sobhy and lamentable economic situation. The Government had to chalkout effective plannings, schemes, prospects and programmes to eradicate poverty from the country which had taken perpetual shape. This again required huge amount of finance and technical skill to give effect to the policies and programmes in this regard. There was also a need to fight decisively with the native forces who wanted a capitalistic India to serve their ends.

During the British administration in India the administrative pattern was based on the principle of centralisation of powers. Under the East India Company's rule the district collector was the chief administrative authority. Each emphasis was laid down on collection of revenues and maintenance of law and order. Upto the Bentinck's period district administration had no separate officer or functionary to take care of agriculture and other rural subjects. The district collector used to get instructions from the Government and he was solely responsible to the Government only for his performances. The pattern of development administration which was getting place in India during the British rule was, in fact, purely based on the principles of individualism and 'Laissez-faire'. The basic motive of the administration was to protect the individual private property and interests.

Keeping in view the troubles caused by famines and draughts to the general masses, the British Government adopted some welfare policies, no doubt, but these were all based on humanitarian point of view. There was no plan or policy to accelerate rural upliftment. The Government simply distributed certain reliefs among the sufferers. Later on, realisation came to the Government that until there was executive interference in the affairs of the free and private enterprises, the administration could not deal with the selfish and vested elements whose sole objective was to enrich themselves by exploiting the existing situation. The Famine Commission (1880) had also recommended the Government to go for organising rural administration for proper execution of the welfare policies of the Government towards rural people.

Lord Curzon, who was very much interested in giving sound administrative pattern in India, did a lot in this regard. He created the Department of Agriculture with a view to making basic changes in the agricultural products and improving the position and prospects of the farmers. Warren Hasting contributed to the district administration by making the planning of a uniform system of district administration. The Royal Commission of Decentralisation (1907) recommended for reconstitution of village panchayat system in India with the power to deal with certain small cases in the villages and to supervise the developmental rural works including the schools etc. In the Government of India Act, 1919 some provisions for village panchayats were incorporated, but due to non-cooperation movement this trial could not be given to these provisions.

It was Lord William Bentinck who recognised first time that no modernization could take place in India until the local people of India were allowed to take share in their own development. He analysed the situation and realised that no efforts were applied to bring change in the rural structure through reviving Indian society from within the infrastructure. So he took the initiative to do something decisively for local development in India. Thereafter Lord Mayo set up rural boards under the scheme of decentralisation of powers in 1870 with a view to administering local funds provided by the Government for local administration. No doubt, scope was made for the local representatives in these Local Boards but, in the beginning, nearly fifty per cent of the members of the Boards were Government servants. The policy of local self-Government in India during the British administration had two objectives. Firstly, there was an intention to build a provincially reinforced local fund in order to free imperial finance as from local functions, and secondly, reconstruction of local bodies so as to provide additional avenues for educated employment and keep the politically motivated elites engaged in the exercise of a measure of power, influence and authority.

Several Presidencies in India set up Local Boards or Rural Boards which became responsible for local administration as well as local welfare and development. Some changes in regard to structural framework and powers of these bodies were made to make them more effective. Before 1919, there was no remarkable progress in the functioning of these bodies. The purposes for which these bodies were set up could not be realised. The main reason for their unsatisfactory performances was the dominant authority of the government over them and less participation of the local people. Those local representatives who participated in these bodies were not the real representatives of the general masses. Rather they belonged to the classes of the vested interests or the persons of high influence belonging to the upper strata of the society.

Policies, plannings and infrastructure for rural administration and rural development took place in India after Independence in real sense. The Indian leaders had fully realised even before independence that it was not possible to alter the socio-economic structure of the Indian society unless some decisive steps were taken in this regard. So it was decided that to develop the rural society of India the Planning Commission of the country must initiate to make appropriate plans for rural development on the one hand and the village panchayat system should be reorganised on the democratic principles on the other. So the Planning Commission took up responsibility in this regard and became busy with finding solution to the problems of poverty and rural development.

The Government of free India under the leadership of the Congress Party headed by Pt. Jawaharlal Nehru thought of the 'Community Development Programme' as the most suitable model for rural development in India. This programme was launched all over the country covering rural areas where the Block Development Officer with a team of Extension Officers, Village-Level Workers and other staff are to play vital roles for rural development. The Government also appointed some committees like Balwant Rai Mehta Committee and Ashok Mehta Committee to suggest measures for reorganising the Village Panchayat System. Basing on the reports of these committees, the Government began the three-tier panchayati raj which have become most reliable institutions for rural development all over India.

The Planning Commission of India, in the beginning, did not pay much attention to the local level planning for rural development. Its main thrust was towards expansion of heavy industries and agricultural development. For more than a decade planning remained purely an arithmetical exercise at the national level with emphasis on "heavy industries, major and medium irrigation and heavy machinery mostly feeding urban industrial complexes." No doubt, there were some plans for rural development during the early phase of planning in India. But the main beneficiaries of the planning in the rural areas were affluent farmers who have the resources to obtain modern agricultural inputs.

The Government of India began to adopt various schemes and projects for the removal of poverty from the rural areas from the Fourth and Fifth Five Year Plans. The local development machinery was constructed on the democratic principles where the local population got opportunity to take direct part in the process of installing village panchayats, Anchal Parishad or Samiti and Zila Parishad. The Planning Commission became more interested in preparing plans for rural development. Emphasis was laid on district level planning. It was realised that the district was still not an ideal unit of planning for the purpose and that the method of planning was also defective. It was also realised that the mobilisation of local raw material, human resources and all decentralised economic activities such as agriculture, minor irrigation, rural industries, health, education and other social facilities required a smaller area approach. So the Community Development Blocks were considered ideal for this purpose because they are much smaller than districts. So the efforts were applied to prepare plannings from the Block Level where villages would play vital role in preparing and implementing the plans at the grass-root level. Blocks also provide the area base where various sectoral plans sponsored by the Centre or the State can be integrated to the maximum. Block level planning has also been found the appropriate system of planning as a natural corollary of the system of administration reaching down the district from the top. Keeping in view the above mentioned facts, the policy-makers and planners of India gave too much preference to the Community Development Programmes all over the country based on the concept of decentralised local planning.

With the main cry of the Government to the slogans like 'Garibi Hatao' and 'Berozgari Hatao' the Government, specially from seventies of the last century adopted numerous Community Development Programmes, poverty-alleviation programmes and programmes to provide self-employment in the rural areas. The programmes, like Small Farmers Development Agency, Marginal Farmers and Agricultural Labour Development Agency, Cash Employment Programme, Minimum Need Programme etc. soon appeared with a view to helping the poor sections of the society. All these programmes were poverty alleviation programmes. The Government under the leadership of Mrs. Indira Gandhi took-up all the possible steps to first the national finance towards the rural areas specially among the poor sections through these programmes.

During the Fifth and Sixth Five Year Plans various programmes and schemes were introduced all over the country for poverty alleviation and raising the living standard of the rural people. But desired results could not be achieved. It was all because of sectoral approach to the planning. The real benefits did not reach to the real poor sections of the society. Rather these programmes enabled the afluent classes to obtain the benefits. The poor sections of the society remained still far away from the benefits of the rural development programmes. Moreover, these programmes were effective only in the areas where Blocks had been set up. So there was regional disparities in development. There were various agencies which were separately operative without any inter-link among themselves. Therefore, realisation came that there should be single integrated development programme to be called as Integrated Rural Development Programme (IRDP). This programme covered all aspects of the rural life all over the country.

The IRDP stands today to be the Government's single largest anti-poverty thrust. All other programmes like Community Development Project, Small Farmer Development Agency, Small Marginal Farmer Development Agency, Draught Prone Area Project, C.A.D.A. etc. were ad hoc in nature and time bound. With the emergence of the IRDP all these programmes and projects merged together under the !RDP. The IRDP is the core of the new plan strategy and in scope goes much beyond the earlier rural development programmes. Thereafter a new scheme, namely, Jawahar Rojgar Yojana (JRY) appeared with the object to provide more employment opportunities to the rural labour class.

The policy and steps of the Government of India to change the rural face, help the downtrodden and suppressed sections of the people in their upliftment and provide ample opportunity to the rural poor were very much appreciable. The government has invested a huge amount of money to achieve the purpose. It is true that some markable success has been achieved in this regard all over the country. Such policy and steps of the government have created new feeling and hope in the mind of the poor Indians. But the most important thing is to note that the achievement of the objectives fixed by the government through the rural development plans and schemes are not much encouraging. The channelization of the amount of funds towards the rural side has yielded some bad trends. It has resulted in misappropriation of the government fund and encouraged mass corruption among both the government servants and the general public. The schemes of rural development have been exploited by the vested interests at the cost of the poor. Hence there is a need to make a fresh and deep study of all these developing trends in the schemes sponsored by the Government of India from a new angle. For this, the Indian administrative structure related to rural development and a new administrative changes to give albeit to the rural development of the rural people should also be analysed properly. There is also a need to investigate and analyse the factors responsible for creating hindrances on the path of rural administration. The present work is an exercise in this respect.

The First Chapter namely, Rural India and its People, gives an elaborate description of the people and their economic condition before and after arrival the British in India. In fact, the rural population of India was drowned in mass poverty facing acute scarcity. The British ruled them but did nothing for their economic development. The chapter also discusses the cruel excessivenesses committed by the Indian Landlords and the Zamindars upon the rural people.

After Independence the Government of India made certain changes in rural administrative framework for rural development. A new and novel project called the Community Development Project (CDP) was launched in some selected areas. The Second Chapter studies and the objectives of the CDP and critically analyses the achievement and failure of the CDP. The Third Chapter presents a detail study of the policies of the Government in Regard to Rural Development. It also studies the objectives behind such governmental policies. And effort has been made to observe the administrative changes which the Government of India brought for rural development.

Chapter Fourth, namely, Integrated Rural Developments Programmes: A Review, is an exercise to investigate into various schemes and projects of the government under integrated plans and programmes to change the socio-economic structure of the rural people. The government initiated a country-wide popular programme known as the IRDP with the objective to remove mass poverty from the rural field. The IRDP covered all aspects of the rural life all over the country. This chapter presents a detail account of the IRDP and analysis its merits and demerits.

The Government of India launched some more rural employment programme and rural landless guarantee programme covering the whole country. Chapter Fifth, discusses and examines the Objectives and Effectiveness of these programmes.

The Government of India under Rajiv Gandhi was fully determined to provide some more economic opportunities to the poorest of the poor specially in the rural areas. Hence the government continuing the programme under IRDP, launched a new Yojana, namely, the Jawahar Rojgar Yojana (JRY) with a view to create new avenues of employment for the rural labourers. Chapter Sixth studies objectively and examines deeply the objectives of JRY and its implementation.

The last chapter, Recent Special Schemes and Agencies for Development of Rural Poor, presents a short descriptive and critical account of the recent steps of the Government of India in the field of poverty eradication from the rural areas. It also studies the working of some volunteer agencies with a commitment to help the poor rural mass.

Besides, these seven chapters the work contains Introduction, Conclusion and Bibliography. The method of the study of this project is empirical and analytical based on datas and facts. The approach is objective and purpose is to throw new light on upgradation of socio-economic standard of the rural people specially the downtrodden, depressed, deprived and suppresses sections of the society. The materials have been collected from most reliable sources. In this regard both original and secondary sources have been utilised. The view points of several relevant public leaders, political leaders, scholars etc. have also been obtained through personal interviews with them. To make the work more reliable and objective, several areas where the rural development schemes and projects have been running, have also been studied and served personally.

The purpose of this research is to investigate and analyse the works of the governmental and non-governmental agencies which have remained responsible for implementing the policies and the programmes of the government. The changes in the level of the employment and income, the expenditure and saving pattern of the people have been assessed. No doubt, some important studies have been made in this regard by both the government and private organisations. Some books have also been written by some notable authors on the issues. But these studies and books do not present a study of coherrent whole of the rural development of India. Moreover, their description and analysis is not related to the administrative changes in this regard. That is why the present work is an exercise to study this and answer some relevant questions related to rural development. It appears that the purposes of the research have been achieved.

1

Rural India and Its People

India is basically rural innature where majority of the people reside in villages. It is true that due to rise and growth of urbanization and industrialisation several cities and numerous terms which have recently appeared, have attracted rural population in a search of new jobs and professions. But it does not mean that Indian society has fully been industrialised. Reality is that rural society is still the base of the Indian population. The socio-economic history of India before the arrival of the British in the country, reveals the story of mass poverty, distress and starvation of the people belonging to the lower stratum of the society. The society itself was based on deep rooted superstitions and dogmatic religious practices. When Renaissance dawned in Europe at the beginning of the modern age, India was a sleeping giant, the caste system which widely prevailed in the Hindu community, was the basic criterion of the social structure.[1] Mass illiteracy prevailed everywhere. In absence of education the general people were neither in position to trace out the cause of their poverty and suffering nor in a state to fight with their enemies.

Economically the Indian society was divided into two classes—the rich and the poor. The middle class was yet to apply Rulers, Princes, Nawabs. Countries and vassals belonged to the former class while the peasant, agricultural labourers, urban workers, craftsmen, artisans, petty servants were the main constituents of the latter class. Wealth, privileges, castes and birth were the symbol of dignity and position in the society. "The western notion of equality, liberty and equal opportunity to all irrespective of caste, creed, religion, birth, race and faith were beyond the concept of the existing political consciousness of the people. Mass poverty and illiteracy were the greatest factors of the political backwardness of the masses."[2]

The arrival of the British in India was a turning point in the socio-eco-political history of India. The British ruler brought with themselves in India new political philosophy and new technologies. They also established new schools and colleges which soon began to impart the western education. Though only rich people in India could afford the expenditure to get into the higher educational institutions and have higher knowledge, the English education began to change the traditional and superstitious concept and attitude of the Indians.

It is true that the basic idea behind introducing English institutions in India was to prepare a class to assist the British rulers in India. The British were exploiters. However, some of the British administrators paid the attention to the rural field and provided new set of administration to help the rural people. The Indian rural society's economy was self-sufficient and stable due to limited needs of the people. But the British administration spoiled the self-sufficiency of the rural India. The fall of the Mughal Empire had paved the way for the feudal aristocracy while the rule of the East India Company strengthened the position of the Indian landlords, who became the intermediaries between the rulers and the tillers. It was Warren Hasting, the then Governor-General of Bengal, who allowed the landlords to collect rent from the cultivators on commission. Thereafter, Lord Cornwallis, proceeding one step ahead by introducing the Permanent Settlement Act of 1793 in Bengal made the landlords real sovereign of lands. The Act permitted them to appropriate the whole of the rent collected by them after paying the share of the Company.

The landlords who had to pay a share of the rent to the company began to exploit the farmers. To quote Tara Chand "the settlement destroyed and the old village community, changed the property relations, created new social classes and caused a social revolution in the Indian countryside.[3] To quote Tara Chand once more "The law of 1793, on the one hand, opened the flood-gates of exploitation of the helpers peasantry and on the other, confirmed the revenue farmers as absolute proprietor of the estates.[4] In the meanwhile, a new class comprising moneylenders and bhoo-grain merchants also appeared with a view to exploit the peasantry class by lending money to them on high rate of interest and buying their products very cheap.

The farmers had to serve two masters at a time. On the one hand, they had to pay the Landlords or Zamindars, on the other, they had also to please the workers of the Zamindars. Whenever the cultivators failed to pay the *dustury* (a sort of established tax), he had to meet harsh and cruel punishment which included, "lash, chain, imprisonment and confiscation of his property.[5] More over his land was put on auction in case he failed to pay the rent to the landlords in time. Thus all they broke the backbone of the Indian peasantry class. Henry Thomas Colebrook, an English author and authority of the East India Company who had personally surveyed the rural areas of Bihar, Bengal, Orissa and Allahabad wrote that "we cannot then wonder and the signs of distress which this class of cultivators exhibit, nor that they are often compelled by accumulating debts, to emigrate from province to province."[6] One more English Traveller, Bishop Hober who made a tour to the rural areas in 1824-1825, noted down in his history that "During the wet months they (the rural poor) can be scooped up with a hand-net in every field and procured at all times of the expense of a crooked vail and a little plantain thread... except food, in such a climate their wants are but few, very little clothing serves and even this is worn more for a decency than necessity. They have no furniture, except a cane bedstead or two, and some copper pots."[7]

Under the new land system "exploitation and conservation of waste-land pastures, fisheries and forests ceased to be regulated by custom and became subject to the new landlord's right to private property."[8] This tempted the moneylenders and foodgrain merchants. They developed more interest in rural economy and soon succeeded in becoming the owner of more than half of the village land. The introduction of the *Ryotwari* system in other parts of the country in the early part of last century" pulled down the level of living of the rural poor, while grinding poverty and competition for land were independent factors depressing the average level of productivities in the agricultural economy."[9] Describing the effect of the new *Ryotwari* land system Bourlillon, a British contemporary author said that a ryot "is always in poverty and generally in debt. He lives from hand to mouth and rarely sees money. His dwelling is a hut of mud walls and thatched roof, far ruder and smaller and dilapidated than those of the better classes of ryots. His food and that of his family is partly thin porridge made of the meal of grain boiled in water and partly boiled rice with a little condiments."[10] Again describing the condition of a labourer he wrote that in respect of "food, house and clothing the labourer is in a worse condition than the class of a poor ryots. Almost the whole of his earning must necessarily be consumed in spare allowance of coarse and unvaried food and a bare sufficiency of clothing. The wretched hut he lives in can hardly be valued at all."[11]

Raja Ram Mohun Roy, the father of modern India, after assuring the agrarian structure during the British period, came to the conclusion that the new land system made by the British helped the landlords and the moneylenders to grow rich while the condition of the actual tillers went on worsening.[12] He maintained that "whatever it was, permanent settlement or Ryotwari settlement, the condition of the cultivators was very miserable" because, "under the former system they were placed at the mercy of Zamindars, avarice and ambition," while under the latter "they were subjected to the extortion and intrigues of the surveyors and other Government Revenue Officers."[13]

Thus it is evident that with the beginning of the British rule in India especially in the agrarian field the miseries and troubles of the Indian peasants as well as the agricultural labourers increased to a great extent. Ganguli has rightly observed: "Indian agrarian structure developed into an exploitative system that impoverished the poor masses, inhibited progress and sustained the low level of living of the bulk of the population."[14] It is true that the policies were formulated by the government for rural development on the suggestions given by the zamindars, but the latter were hardly interested in development. Most of them were found of luxuries and comforts for which they left no stone unturned to exploit the poor farmers. There was hardly any development schemes. Moreover, there was political and administrative uncertainty.

The British East India Company which arrived in India with a view to developing commercial relations and spreading western trades in India received the diwani of Bengal, Bihar and Orissa in 1765. This was, in fact, an assignment which invested the Company with the civil administration of the districts. As the company itself was interested in money making, it hardly worked for development. Rather it tried all the best to maintain status quo ante. During the regime of Warren Hasting, in 1772, the Collectors were appointed by the Company to supervise the works of the Zamindars in regard to revenue administration. But no change could be marked in development administration. It is evident from the sixth report of the Committee of Secrecy of the House of Commons. The Report pointed out that every zamindari and taluk was left to its own peculiar customs and these too were not invialably adhered to. The Zamindars got the opportunity to enrich themselves at the cost of the poor and also of the Company's shares. It was said that the Zamindars and the other landlords who had the advantage of long possessions, availed themselves of it by complex divisions of the lands, intricate modes of collection, to perplex the officers of the government, and confine the knowledge of the rents to themselves. It will be easily imagined that much of the current wealth stopped in the way to the public treasury."[15] Thus it is clear that the Zamindars and their allied groups of landholders as a class continued to do everything possible to preserve the commanding influence before the East India Company took over the administration of the country.

The Company under the Dewani rule took a severe measures to ascertain the revenue and also to protect the interests of the peasants. When Hasting was appointed as the Governor of Bengal, he took up some special measures to improve the situation. He thought that until the sovereign power was exercised by the Company, it was impossible to make remarkable changes in the development administration in India. The trouble was that the Company were not yet ready to go to such an extent. As a result upto 1781 no fixed pattern of district administration could be established. However, during 1774-49 several districts were separated from the provincial councils and formed into distinct collectorship on a different footing.[16] While the Amending Act (1781) recognised the legislative authority of the Company's Supreme Government in Bengal and reduced the power of the Supreme Court, Pitt's India Act (1784) provided for parliamentary control over the Company's India affairs in a manner which continued with certain changes till 1858.

Following the foot print of Warren Hasting in the field of administration, Sir John Shore, an able civil servant, pressed for the introduction of a uniform principle of administration and recommended that a covenated servant of the Company should be appointed to every district with powers to administer both revenue and civil justice.[17] The recommendation of Sir Shore got support and the Company's directors finally accepted it keeping in view that the executive authority of Government and the Company's own sovereignty could not be strengthened except by the vigour of the European agency of covenated servants.[18] So the Directors asked the Governor General-in-Council to place all the districts in the hands of their convenated servants under the title of Collectors.[19] The Directors were authorised to appoint or dismiss their Indian subordinates subject only to information being submitted to the Committee of Revenue at Calcutta which was established on the abolition of the provincial councils in 1781. Thus the revenue and civil justice both came under the British servants on the justification of simplicity of administration. Soon the collectors became more powerful in the field of administration. In the place of indigenous *faujdar* magistracy was created and united with the office of the collector of the district. Consequently, the District Collector in addition to the immediate function of revenue collection and rural relief he became judge and magistrate, too.

In the beginning the British East India Company made district collector the chief administrative authority. Each district was divided into some Talukas and Parganas and put under the charge of some officers. But it is interesting to note that the company failed to deal with the landlords properly with the result that they still remained as the parasites and the farmers and the workers of India suffered under two masters—the foreigners and the indigenous. The immediate and main concern of the company government was to reconstitute the administration of districts which, on the decline of the Mughals had, either disintegrated or become dysfunctional. It was natural that this reconstitution should have taken place in the first instance to ensure a due discharge of the state's regulatory functions, the functions of executive and judicial administration, with an emphasis on the collection of the public revenues and maintenance of law and order. Before the abolition of the Company's trade in 1833 the scope of district administration remained largely limited to these functions. Since the development administration largely depends upon the district administration, it is well to have the knowledge of district administration during the British period which became basic district administrative pattern of India even after Independence of the country. Upto the Lord Bentinck's period the Collector-Magistrate, the District Judge and the Civil Surgeon were the superior officers in the administration of the district. Though predominantly rural in setting, district administration had no separate officer to take care of agriculture. It was the duty of the Collector to remain in touch with the ryots, to induce them to bring waste best areas into cultivation. It was also the duty of the District Collector to take necessary measures to develop agriculture and protect the farmers during the days of natural calamities such as flood, draught etc. It was he who was authorised to protect the farmers, workers and other people of the poor sections from the exploitation of the landlords. In fact, the

District Collector assumed the most honourable and responsible place among the people. He had the power of supervision of every branch of civil executive business. It was that supervisory power "which invests him in the eyes of the people with the position of the local head of the civil Government.[20]

The District Collectors used to get instructions and guidance from the higher Government through different departments. They used to send reports to the superior authorities for information and formulation of policies in the district. There were some subordinate civil servants under the District Collector whose main duty was to assist the Collector in administration. In the beginning, no Indian was allowed to come in the realm of appointment of the civil services with the result that they remained out of the structure of the civil service in India. English was the main problem in this regard. But with the introduction of English teaching in India and alertness and demands the Indian people the gate of entry in the civil services were opened for the Indians, too. Improvement occurred with the progress of higher education, but it was not before 1892.[21]

It can be noted here that the pattern of development administration which was getting place in India during the British Raj was based upon the line of capitalism which itself was based on the principles of individualism and 'Laiseez-faire'. Both the British administrators and the Indian well-to-do class were much inclined towards capitalism with the result that little attention was paid to public welfare. Dr. Mishra has rightly observed that the educated public opinion in India as well as the bureaucracy encouraged Europeans to settle as capitalists.[22] In the words of Misra "It was this class of colonizers who urged the Company's government to improve India's communications and introduce railways to facilitate the movement of trade in commercial crops and agricultural produce. It was they who provided incentives to the establishment of 'special departments' to support the extention of free enterprise, specially in the rural areas where the exigencies of the colonial economy dicted the need not only of road and building construction, but also of irrigational, medical and public health facilities. They served as a primary instrument of rural development, though not in a positive sense."[23]

The British liberated the business enterprise from the official control and restrictive barriers which enabled the alert and conscious Indians to take the benefit of the circumstance. It were they who getting the benefit of the opportunity emerged as the middle class of India and preferred the capitalist system of administration. They "emerged in course of time as an organised pressure group in India, influencing both Central and Local Governments to enact measures, the economic benefits of which extended likewise to the afluent Indian landed and commercial classes. They developed in fact an identity of interest between them and emerging Indian middle classes in business and other fields that brought David Yule, the Chairman of the Bengal Chamber of Commerce, to over the annual session of the Indian National Congress in 1888."[24]

Thus the basic principle of the Indian administration remained confined to the protection of individual private property and interests. "The complexities of Indian Constitution of courts, their procedural sophistication and the codification of laws were all evidence of the concern which the Government of India felt for the promotion of that efficiency."[25] The British Indian Association and the Indian Association which were formed by alert and educated Indians as pressure groups also favoured the middle class economy. They represented the views of aristocracy and the educated middle class in various ways and fields. The protection and development of the lower section of the society remained the subject matter of the District Collector or District Magistrate. The theoretical aspects of development administration inclined towards the western side which was individualistic in nature and spirit. As a result, nothing could be done remarkably for the development of the poor during the first phase.

Rural development in the context of development administration in India mainly signifies the development of agriculture and as such other elements as are of immediate relevance to the welfare of the rural population. The first phase of rural development under the British began with the administration of revenue itself. Apprehensive schemes of land survey also provided opportunity for the rural development in India. The surveys and settlement operations which Collectors had to undertake as part of their immediate duties furnished information which constituted a basis for agricultural policy, land reforms and measures for agricultural improvement.

From 1770 onwards India suffered from continuous famines which drew the attention of the government. The importance of agriculture as the mainstay of the rural economy and the direct responsibility of the state to promote it, came to be specially realised as a raesult of a series of famines that occured in the different parts of the country. The Famine Commission of India which made the survey of the rural areas submitted its report in 1880 and suggested certain viable measures to protect the rural people and improve the agriculture.[26]

The idea of rural development through the government under the British administration was initially a search for an alternative of Laissez faire, a profit-based economic principle which had failed to provide relief to famine-stricken people and necessitated some bureaucratic intervention in restricting free trade. The new attitude towards rural development found expression mainly in two directions—firstly, a reorganization of the internal administrative arrangement, and secondly, a delegation of some responsibility to self governing local bodies. The former included, for example, a move towards the establishment of a separate department of agriculture at the Centre and in the Provinces, a scheme of financial decentralization to enable Provinces to find means to promote their own development work in the various technical departments, the organisation of a number of All-India specialized services to ensure uniformity and efficiency in the direction and supervision of technical department in the Provinces, and finally, an attempt to provide some kind of training in agriculture for Indian Civil Services. All these steps were taken on the suggestion tendered by the Famine Commission. It was the Commission which encouraged the government to go for development administration.

No doubt, the government took some steps to improve the rural areas to increase the agricultural produce and obtain more economic gain. But an important in the concept of rural development was a humanitarian welfare approach to administration. In the beginning, the Company's Government had no concern towards welfare of the rural population. In 1858, the rule of the East India Company was over, and India came under the rule of the British Empire directly. Before the report submitted by the Famine Commission of India in 1880, the country had badly suffered from famines where millions of people had lost their lives. But the Government could not budge even a single inch from its old conservative ideas. The Report of the Famine Commission states that "The view then adopted were that the main duty of Government was to offer employment to those who could work, but that the relief of the helpless and infirm members of the population was the business of the charitable public... where the pressure on these charitable funds was exceptionally great, some assistance was given from the treasury, but not as a matter of right."[27]

Thus it is obvious that there was no place at all for welfare administration. It was emphasized that able bodied labourers employed in relief works be paid "at a low rate of daily wages, a fixed task of work being demanded in returns."[28] As welfare-based gratuity was no part of the concern of the Government, relief was "carried on at the expense of the charitable public, added by contributions from other parts of India and from England; it was generally distributed in the form of cooked food to persons who submitted to the condition of residence in an enclosed poor house."[29] The suffering was great and charity was less with the result that many people died due to lack of proper food, cloth and medicine. According to the report of the Civil Surgeon at Cuttack "People died in the roads and fields all about; many died who never seen... In my opinion the cause of excessive mortality was that the people were gone too far before they came in; they all died from starvation, not from sickness in the ordinary sense."[30] The situation caused by the famine was so serious but the Government remained inactive only because there was no humanitarian approach. The Civil Surgeon further noted that "If the relief had been commenced two or three months earlier, thousands of lives might have been saved, but no more seemed to appreciate the gravity of the situation."[31]

People suffered not only from continuous famines but also from epidemics like diarrhoea, cholera, dysentery, fever, opthalmia etc.[32] There was no provision to protect the people from these malandies. The Cholera Commission of 1861 was the first to raise the voice and invite the attention of the government towards the problem. The Royal Army Sanitary Commission, too, came ahead to plead the case of the poor masses. All these factors compelled the government to be sympathetic towards the people and adopt some welfare measures to help them. According to the report of the Famine Commission "It was not laid down for the first time that the object of the Government was to save every life, and that district officers would be held responsible (for ensuring) that no preventable deaths should occur. It was found necessary to depart, in some degree, from the old principle,that it was the duty of the public to provide for the gratuitous relief of the infirm and weak, seeing that so large a proportion of these were foreigners and not the local poor; and the Government declared that it would supplement private subscriptions by whatever sum might be necessary for the support of the persons incapable of work."[33] Thus the welfare schemes of the Government began. The Government now aimed to improve the state of public health by at attempt to prevent loss of life from starvation and check the outbreak of epidemic diseases which used to result due to unhygienic conditions caused by famines. Meanwhile the Christian Missions, too, came ahead enthusiastically to help the people. They raised subsciptions from England and influenced the Government in India to make relief from such private source available. But it can be noted that the relief was still given to those persons who lived in `a poor house' where paupers hesitated to go for fear of a loss of caste.[34]

Once the Government decided to provide welfare to the concerned persons, it initiated some schemes. Tests and restrictions were relaxed in respect of the wages, the amount of work done and the character of the work offered. Provision was also made for sufficient money or grain to sustain. Cultivators were at the same time invited to take loans of money or rise repayable without interest. The step was taken to build up a sufficient reserve when the original purchase was effected so that when the pressure passed this surplus was sold at a loss.[35] These schemes and measures, infact, brought some relief to the poor sections of the people.

The British Government was not yet ready to take all the responsibility to save every distressed persons of the poor sections. The policy of the Government regarding the development administration was to provide "efficient assistance for the suffering people without incurring disastrous expenditure.[36] Matter came to the light that the step taken by the government for storing food grains on cheap rate for the distribution among the starving people had badly affected the policy of the free trade system. It was reported that "very serious and unjustifiable interference with trade caused by disposing of it in various ways at a rate considerably cheaper than the market rate. Not only was the power of trade greatly neutralized, but the people became demoralized and reckless, seeing the extraordinary exertions of government, represented by its officials, to get rid, apparently, of as much grain as possibly by some means or other."[37] Moreover, the relief and loans given to the people were not utilised for the purpose for which these were given. People thought that they would not be asked to refund the loans. It was observed that money advanced even for land improvement or purchase of grain was diverted to other channels.[38]

Despite all these the Government could not make any viable change in its policy.[39] The Famine Commission suggested some more measures in the concept of welfare. These were preventive measures of constant application to counteract the recurrence of agricultural distress or to mitigate its severity in further. These measures, for instance, included provisions for irrigation and rural financing, advances of loans and agricultural statistics, tenurial improvements and agricultural administration. These suggestions were very much significant in that the agricultural classes in India constituted the vast majority of its total population. This helped the farmers and saved them from the periodical occurrence of famine and the appalling distress involved. The period that followed the Commission's report of 1880 was characterized by efforts to apply both the palliative and preventive principles of public welfare.[40]

During the course of time the government realised that the welfare policies and schemes could not be implemented fully without planning and executive control. There was the official dependency on private trade as the only recognized agency of food supply and distribution. The government could not do its duty properly. Due to official dependency on private trade it was not possible to send immediate relief to the concerned people. The grain merchants were great obstacle on the way. They were trying to raise the price of food grains by storing food grains. The artificial scarcity of food grains was created. Some times food grains were not available in the market even at high rate, too. No doubt, suggestion was given to fix the price, but it was impossible because the Collectors denied to do so. It was reported that "It was established principle of government that commerce that is in force in England, shall be accepted in all her dependencies throughout the world, wherever may be their condition and circumstances, and that such a thing was quite out of the question."[41]

The general tendency of the business communities was to exploit the sufferings of the people to a mass wealth. The principle of free trade imported from England proved harmful in Indian society. The local administrators could do nothing in this regard. The views of the Indian Civil Service were as a whole regulated by the contemporary doctrine of laissez faire, a doctrine that was calculated to promote Britain's economic interest in collaboration with Indian traders who used it as a lever to secure freedom from bureaucratic control for their own profiteering purposes.

Secondly, there was, in fact, no planning to meet the drought that fell constantly. According to the report of the Famine Commission (1880) in the absence of any plan to meet the situation caused emergently by droughts "it had to be dealth with by a boy of officials necessarily ignorant of the signs of its approach, unprepared to expect it, and inexperienced in the administration of relief measures."[42]

Realisation came to the government that until the executive was allowed to interfere in the free trade and some preplans were adopted, it was not possible to go ahead with the public welfare policies and save the lives of people. The drought of 1868 in the North-Western Provinces obliged the government to introduce an element of welfare as a guiding principle of famine policy. It enabled the administration to foresee the danger and plan relief measuresin good time to avoid death from starvation and disease. It was, however, the Bihar famine of 1874 that brought into relief the elements of planning and executive control as important instruments of rural welfare. Thereafter, the Secretary of State and the Government of India were both persuaded by the Government of Bengal to use executive interference with free trade as the only means of saving the masses from its deadly grip over the market.[43]

Despite the aforesaid factors, there were some other concepts that were related not only to meeting distress but, more specially to the positive aspects of rural development in terms of agricultural improvement on a continuous basis. These included central directions, statistical information and feedback, and specialization in developmental services involving the knowledge of science and technology. Thus in the words of B.B. Misra "Famines in India not only provided a conceptual frame of reference, but also dictated the necessity of administrative action based on the concepts so developed. Ultimately, this promoted rural development, especially agriculture."[44]

The Government wanted to investigate into the conditions of agricultural field in India on the suggestions given by the Bengal and Orissa Famine Commission in 1866. To achieve the purpose it was thought to constitute the agricultural departments at both the central and provincial level. The order was given by the Secretary of State to establish a special branch in the administrative framework which primary functions were to collect from villages records such statistics and information as might though light on questions of agriculture, including the economic resources of the country, and then to suggest measures for the development of agricultural industry.[45] Consistent with this object the first step taken was the formation in 1871 of a new branch of the central secretariat to deal with the general scheme of agricultural development as part of the department of revenue and commnerce.

In 1875, the provincial department of agriculture was created in North-Western Provinces. At the central level, before the creation of agricultural department, Home, Revenue and Agriculture were amalgamated together which created inconveniences for agricultural growth. So a new department of agriculture was created which duties were:

(i) A complete and systematic inquiry into vital agricultural and economic information for every part of India,

(ii) The general improvement of Indian agriculture, with the view of increasing the food supply and general resources of the people, and

(iii) A better and prompter organisation of famine relief whenever the actual approach of famine might be indicated by the statistical information available with the officers of Government."[46]

To achieve the aforesaid objectives the Famine Commission had also recommended for creation and expansion of a very elaborate local machinery functioning under the supervision and control of the provincial departments of agriculture. It was recommended to open agricultural science and to include agricultural services under the Indian Civil Services. Further suggestion was given to maintain land records at village level so that correct statistics could be collected.

The improvement in the agrarian fields depends on the local machinery of the government. So the Famine Commission had too much emphasis on building the local self-Government all over the provinces. The Commission viewed that success in agricultural inquiry would depend mainly on the completeness and accuracy which the agricultural, vital and compiled in each sub-division and district throughout the country. It was, therefore, considered necessary that the institution of village accountants be reformed and revived, and they should be put under effective supervision in each district under the control of a Deputy Collector whose main or only "duty would be to take charge of all matters connected with the economic condition and well-being of the people.[47] This special officer was to test and compile the agricultural returns, to examine the market prices and ascertain from these and order data the relative value of each year's crop, according to whether it was below or above the average.

No doubt, the Deputy Collector was placed under the Collector but he had to function separately under the command and control of the provincial agricultural department. In the general disciplinary control he was under the Collector of the District, but in technical matters he was to be guided by the provincial department of Agriculture presided over by a Director of Agriculture who was to be the executive head of the agriculture. Moreover, there was a corresponding officer to perform analogous duties under the Government of India in order to assist him in his duties dealing with the local governments in their Departments of Agriculture.[48]

It is notable here that opposition came to the idea and formation of a separate department of Revenue and Agriculture, and also against the appointment of a Deputy Collector who might take the charge of local agaricultural and revenue affairs at the village level. Specially the Collectors as a class were opposed to any division of their authority in the districts. They viewed the plan of local agency as 'very expensive' and expressed themselves against it on the score of its being very expensive affair. Even the Government of India agreed to the view expressed by the District Collectors and advised the Secretary of State to reject the Famine Commission's recommendations in this regard. It was argued that creation of a new agricultural department would involve "a departure from so kind principles of district administration" as the role sought to be assigned to the special statistical officer "was one of the highest and most essential functions of the Chief District Officer."[49] It was further argued that the comprehensive nature of the agricultural, vital and economic inquiries assigned to the special officer had the risk of his being entitled to interfere in any department. Any idea of sharing with the District Officer in the totality of his executive control over administration was at the time considered wholly unplantable. So the Government of India wrote to the Secretary of State in March 1881 that "We certainly think it would be hazardous either to transfer duties so vital from the hands of the more highly trained and responsible public servant (District Collector) to those of his official inferior (Deputy Collector), or to expose the working of the scheme to all the risks inherent in divided Government."[50]

The Government of India was not opposed to creation of a new Agricultural Department. What it opposed was to create a new department in the district and to minimise the authority of the District Collector. It is evident from the letter of the Government which inter alia said that "Local Agricultural Department may hereafter be constituted at the headquarters of each province, somewhat on the model which has been very successfully adopted in the North-Western Provinces and we are prepared to entertain favourably any such proposal, but we do not think it would be advisable to go beyond this at present in the direction of the creation of a special local agency in the District."[51]

The report of the Famine Commission and Voelcker's Report[52] which was reviewed by a series of agricultural conferences during 1890-96, provided clear guidelines on rural development being the most important remedy for the recurrent failure of crops and the resultant loss of human life. Urgency of the new agricultural department was felt and steps were taken. Thereafter efforts were also applied, though slowly, to initiate the knowledge of science and technology which in turn involved a corresponding change in the old pattern of recruitment and training of civil servants in this direction.

It is evident that it was the problem of famines and starvation of the general mass which compelled the Government of India to think about the rural agricultural problems and take some necessary steps to meet the challenging problems. The Government which was reluctant to development administration in the beginning now became active to expand the development services specially in the rural areas for the advancement of agriculture. When Lord Curzon assumed the charge of Governor-General in India, he became more active to sought permanent solution to the problem. Unfortunately the country faced several severe droughts during this period. He, too, appointed some commissions to suggest ways the means to meet the situation. The famous famine of 1899 covered the United Provinces, the Central Provinces and Bombay causing great damage to the human and animal lives. Lord Curzon himself visited to badly affected areas and opened relief fund to help the people. In a statement to his Legislative Council he reviewed the famine of 1899-1900 as the "greatest and most appelling" calamity that any Indian Government had ever had to face. He said that "It had not been merely a failure of crops, but was accompanies also by a failure of feader and in many tracts by an almost complete extermination of cattle."[53]

Lord Curzon who was very much kind to the Indian famine problem did remarkable jobs to help the people by raising funds and relief works. The local governments were asked to defer relief measures till the signs of distress were clear and to adopt rural works of local importance rather than public works where even those who were able to support themselves got generally admitted to relief. The Government of India initiated several new and helpful schemes. In the words of B.B. Misra "Lord Curzon, in fact, viewed efficiency not merely as a mechanical ordering of public affairs, but as an effective instrument of progress and social service."[54]

Thereafter measures were adopted to increase the gross produce of land by an application of science and to protect the peasantry by tenancy legislation as well as by providing suitable alternatives to rural financing and employment to reduce indebtedness and growing pressure on land. Lord Curzon, abandoning the earlier methods came ahead with new measures and provided an expert agency that was to organise research, open experimental farms and initial agricultural education. The Pusa Institute of agriculture was set-up in Bihar in 1903 to serve the purpose. In 1901 the Inspector-General of Agriculture was appointed supported with an expert staff. Provision was also made for a cryptogamic botanist and an entomologist in addition to an agricultural chemist. For doing research in the field of agriculture a well-equipped laboratory was proposed. In the agricultural education there were two aspects basic rural education and higher collegiate education of a technical nature. Special schools were set up to impart training to the persons.[55]

Thus, the appointment of the Inspector-General of Agriculture marked the establishment of a separate Department of Agriculture at the Centre and the Director of the Pusa Institute and the experts in various fields under the supervision of the Inspector-General created conditions for research and thorough agricultural education. The old agricultural colleges and schools were modified. New agricultural institute were opened with well-equipped materials. Research in the field of agriculture began with new enthusiasm. The agriculture colleges provided for a post-graduate course in agriculture for those who had passed the three years' degree course at provincial colleges. Its staff included, besided the Director and the Agricultural Chemist, an entomologist and Cryptogamic Botanist and a Agricultural Bacteriologist, an Agri-Horticulturist and a Biological Botanist with a suitable complement of assistants, a surveyor, a teacher of physics, mechanics and a veterinary graduate. There was also a Board of Agriculture which comprised all the members of the Agriculture Departments, Heads of the Veterinary Department, the Botanical Survey of India and the Bengal Education Department. It had no executive control but brought together scientific and practical experts of the departments to enable them to arrange a common course of action for agricultural improvement in the country as a whole.

Thus it is evident that development administration in India was suitably organised during the regime of Lord Curzon. The Government of India became kind enough to grant aid to the provincial Governments for development administration. The Secretary of State was instructed to sanction the appointment of a separate Director of Agriculture for each large Province.[56] The officers to be appointed for the Directorate were to be the member of the All-India Services. The Veterinary Department was also set up to deal with cattle breeding and the prevention of cattle diseases.[57]

Lord Curzon who took the initiative to start agricultural Departments in the provinces was of the view that until the provinces were allowed to go ahead with their own agricultural staff and management it was not possible to achieve marvellous success in the field of rural development. He believed that "for its complete attainment each province must possess its own staff, its own institute for research and experiment, in fact, a properly organised agricultural department."[58] He maintained that "it is not sufficient merely to create a Government department for the study of agricultural problem; means must also be provided for bringing results of research to the knowledge of the cultivators of the country. The entire object of the movement is to bring the one class into direct relations with the other, and to utilize the discoveries of science or the results of education for the improvement of the position and propsects of the raiyat."[59]

Development administration in India during the British period, thus, began with the planning of a uniform system of district administration in 1772 at the initiative of Warren Hasting. It was he who created the office of the District Collector. Changes were effected from time to time in the constitution of that office to suit the policy requirements. To make the task of Collector easier attempts were made to reconstitute the districts on a principle that provided elements of social and cultural contiguity.

The District Officer provided relief against petty tyrannies. It was the part of his duties to look after the promotion of agriculture, to help projects for improvement, to administer relief, to recommend suspension or remission of land revenue in the event of natural calamities, to preserve peace among agricultural classes, and in short, to secure the welfare of the whole community living in the district.[60]

The sub-divisional system grew with the extended function of the state especially in the post-mutiny period, to meet the exigencies of relief operation against famines and epidemics—The Sub-divisional system was aided by the erstwhile revenue agencies functioning at a still lower level of such smaller units such as tehsils or talukas whose revenue officers were also invested with the maintenance of law and order within limits. These were all governmental agencies of administration which functioned on the basis of bureaucratic despotism. They all played vital roles to raise local resources for local needs in respect of development activities as roads, sanitation, education, public health and the like.

Before the arrival of the British in India the Indian Village System was as 'little republics' in the sense that they were self-sufficient. But the British revenue and the rent laws altered the old village system radically. The British Commercial capitalism which called for mobility in the transfer of landed property for the promotion of the colonial economic scattered the old village system. The new economic trends was reflected in a series of administrative and judicial reforms which attempted to establish the primacy of law over custom of legislative authority over individual discretion. The collective responsibility of the village headman was destroyed. The government initiated the Chaukidari System in the villages. Provisions were made to associate Panchayats with the management of the Chaukidari System. In the words of B.B. Misra "their (Panchayats') function was infact to be restricted to the preservation of peace, and that through the agency of their traditional village watchmen, the Chaukidars, who were to cease functioning as servants of village communities and become stipendiary servants of the government, under immediate orders of local police officers."[61] Thus the Chaukidars, being the representatives of the British rule, became the masters of the village.

The report of the Royal Commission on Decentralisation (1909) recommended a reconstitution of village panchayats with such powers as the trial of petty cases, the supervision of minor village works, the control of primary schools and the management of fuel and fodder reserves. It also suggested certain financial allocations to enable the village panchayats to accomplish objects of their institutions. Keeping in view the rising current of Indian National Movement in 1915, the Bengal District Administration Committee (1915) recommended that village panchayats should be invested with the supervision and control of the chaukidars within their local limits. Thus realization grew among the people that villages would be reinvested with the supervision and control of the security agencies of Chaukidars as well as certain other functions of a developmental nature. But in reality what the government wanted to do through the village panchayats was to raise finance and keep the villages under the thumb of the British rule.

When the rule of Dyarchy was practiced in India in 1919 onwards efforts were made by the Indian ministers to reconstitute the village Panchayats, but it could not be realised due to rising tension between the British Government and the freedom fighters. As the days of independence came nearer, the Indian leaders began to think about more viable ways and means to improve the rural India through Panchayats System.

References

1. S.V. Rathor, *History of Caste in India* (Jaipur 1979), pp. 111-128.
2. Chandrika Singh, *Socialism in India: Rise, Growth and Perspective* (New Delhi, 1986), p. 17.
3. Tara Chand, *The History of the Freedom Movement of India*, Vol. 1, Publication Division, Information and Broadcasting Ministry, Government of India, New Delhi, 1983, p. 252.

4. *Ibid.*, p. 294.
5. Hollinberg, *The Zamindari Settlement of Bengal*, Vol. 1 (Calcutta 1979), pp. 56-58.
6. H.T. Colebrook, *Remark on Husbandary in Bengal* (2nd Ed.) (Sideng Lee, 1906), p. 103.
7. Regional Hober, *Narrative of a Journey through the Upper Provinces of India*, 1824-1825, Vol. 2, (Philadelphia), pp. 247-48.
8. B.N. Ganguli, D.B. Gupta, *Level of Living in India*, (New Delhi 1976), p. 228.
9. B.N. Ganguli & D.B. Gupta, *Level of Living in India*, op. cit., p. 229.
10. *Ibid.*, pp. 229-30.
11. *Ibid.*, p. 230.
12. Susobhan Chandra Shanker (ed), *Ram Mohun Roy and Indian Economy*, compiled on behalf of Socio-Economic Research Institute, (Calcutta, 1965), pp. 12-13.
13. Quoted in B.N. Ganguli's *Level of Living in India*, op. cit., p. 232.
14. *Ibid.*, p. 232.
15. Sixth Report of the Committee of Secrecy of House of Commons, Vol. IV, p. 301A.
16. B.B. Misra, *Judicial Administration of East India.*
17. B.B. Misra, *Central Administration of East India Company, 1773-1834,* Ibid., pp. 128-30.
18. *Ibid.*, p. 132.
19. *Ibid.*
20. *Report of the Indian Commission.*
21. B.B. Misra, *District Administration and Rural Development*, Ibid., p. 64.
22. *Ibid.*
23. *Ibid.*, p. 65.
24. B.B. Misra, *The Indian Middle Class*, (New Delhi, 1974), pp. 104-07.

25. B.B. Misra, *The Administrative History of India 1834-1947*, (New Delhi), pp. 538-64.
26. *Famine Commission Report* (Delhi, 1880), Part-I, Para 72, p. 25.
27. *Famine Commission Report*, (Delhi, 1880), op. cit., Part-I, Para 47.
28. *Ibid.*
29. *Ibid.*, Part-I, para 49.
30. Extract taken from the Report of the Commission Appointed to Enquire into the Famine of Bengal and Orissa, No. 74.
31. *Ibid.*
32. *Ibid.*
33. *Famine Commission Report* (1880), Part-I, Para-55.
34. *Ibid.*, Para-55.
35. *Ibid.*, PartI, Para-57.
36. *Famine Commission Report* (1880), Part-I, Para-61.
37. *Famine Commission Bengal Replies*, Agriculture Branch, Revenue Department, Darjeeling, 5th July, 1878.
38. *Ibid.*, p. 173.
39. *Ibid.*, p. 185.
40. Extract taken from the Summary of the Administration of Lord Curzon... in the Department of Revenue and Agriculture, p. 3.
41. Report of the Famine Commission (1880), Vol. I, p. 337, (Extracts).
42. Extract taken from the Report of the Commissioners appointed to enquire into the Famine in Bengal and Orissa in 1866, p. 13.
43. *Ibid.* Para-57, p. 16.
44. B.B. Misra, *District Administration and Rural Development*, op. cit., p. 83.
45. A. Voelker, *Improvement of Indian Agriculture*, Abstract of Report, p. 462.
46. Home (Public), Progs, July, 1881, No. 19 of 1881. Also see State of Government of India, No. 55, Revenue-I, June, 1881.

47. *Famine Commission Report* (1880), Para-124, Part-I in Home (Public) Progs. July, 1881, N. 31.

48. Ibid., Para-125. No. 31.

49. Home (Public) Progs. July, 1861, No. 199 Para-4 of the Letter.

50. Ibid.

51. The Famine Commission of 1880 was sent in India by the Government of England in 1878 to study the problem of famine in India. After, hectic tours all over the country, it submitted its report to the Government of India in 1880. It was this Commission which had suggested numerous measures to stop famine in India and improve the agricultural produce.

52. Dr. J.A. Voelekar was the Agricultural Chemist of the Royal Agricultural Society who came to India in 1890. He made district analysis for the purpose of rural development and agriculture. He dealt mainly with the projected scheme of agricultural investigation urged by the Famine Commission. Agreeing with the Famine Commission, he reported that the revenue system in the greater part of British India is such as to present unvalid means of ascertaining in the fullest manner all necessary facts relating to agriculture, but that those means have nowhere been completely utilised of made as efficient as they might be.

    See J.A. Voelekar, *Report on the Improvement of Indian Agriculture*, 2nd ed., p. 462.

53. Summary of the Administration of Lord Curzon, January, 1899 to April 1904, p. 3, Para-4.

54. B.B. Misra, *District Administration and Rural Development*, op. cit., p. 106.

55. Summary of the Administration of Lord Curzon, Part-I, p. 13.

56. *Ibid.*, Part-II, Chapter III, Para-2.

57. *Ibid.*, Part-II, Chapter III, Para-8, p. 50.

58. *Ibid.*, Part-I, Para-16, p. 11.

59. *Ibid.*

60. B.B. Misra, "Evolution of the Office of Collector", in *Indian Journal of Public Administration*, (Calcutta), July-September, 1965.

61. B.B. Misra, *Government and Bureaucracy in India*, (Delhi, 1986), pp. 341-42.

2

Administrative Framework for Rural Development during the British Rule

The administrative pattern for rural development in India before the arrival of the British was tradition bound with the sole objective to collect revenues and keep balance in cart-ridden society. There was hardly any established praisian to do public welfare or develop the rural areas. However, the rural society was self-sufficient maintain minimum economic needs of the people. Besides cultivation, the rural people had various types of small scale village industries such as weaving, carpentary, blacksmithy, goldsmithy, goat rearing, sheep-raring etc. Though their living standard was lamentable, they had enough means to earn daily brea. The economic structure of the rural as well as of the urban areas took notable turn soon after the establishment of the rule of the British East India Company. The British who reached India in the guise of traders with a view to spreading their commercial relations, applied all the possible diplomatic and political strategies to take away the political powers from the Mughal rulers in their hands. And they succeeded easily due to political disintegration of India and internal rivalaries among the native rulers.

The Acts and Regulations which the rulers of the East India Company adopted during early period of its rule, were mostly based on the principle of maximum gain and little expenditure. Their chief objective was to exploit the Indian economy and earn the profit. Hence they paid little attention to general public welfare. However, for administrative control in the rural areas, they constituted the administrative unit, namely, the District Board giving it enough authority to collect revenues and keep control over the rural mass with a view to attracting the attention of the people towards the British rule and bringing charges in established traditional rural administration, the company further adopted some new welfare policies and schemes which, in fact, caused major change in the socio-economic structure of rural India.

Under the expansionist policy of Lord Wellesley (1798-1805) the company's territory expanded.[1] The company's policies the administrative measures were broadened for the growth and expansion of modernity in the fields of economic and politics both. Economically, it contributed through records of rights to the growth of mobility in the transfers of lands to a degree that induced investment for purpose of large-scale colonial and capitalist enterprise. Politically, it led to the evolution of a separate legislative authority that gradually "Suppressed custom by law, a new development where the determination of rights to property came to be vested in courts which stated making serious incursions into the erstwhile domain of custom based village communities and cost pavoliayap."[2]

Lord William Bentinck was the first man who made comprehensive contribution to the land records and reforms. It was he who had remarked that no modernisation could take place in India except through Europeans, and that there was little room for change from within the infrastructure of indigenous institutions. As she believed, no efforts were applied to bring change in the rural structure through reviving Indian society from within the infrastructure. The educational policy which the British introduced did not aim to prepare the rural masses and the village communities for local self-governments. Rather it sought to produce through English education a middle class of elites and interpreters who might in subordiante positions assist the British in administration of the country.[3] The education which the British introduced in India was an urban and job-oriented educational policy, with exclusive emphasis on secondary and higher education. However, a shift came in educational policy only afer the Sepoy Mutiny which stated that "Government expenditure should be mainly directed to the provision of elementary education for the mass of the people."[4] But it was too late now.

The need for constitutions of local bodies was felt by the British administrators and rulers as means to raise local funds from the local resources. B.B. Misra also agrees to the point that "the administration of `local fund' necessitated the creation of what came to be known as rural boards or local bodies in the districts. The funds formed part of land revenue in most cases, a source of income which the old village community once used for the promotion of protective and rural welfare services. The European Collectors who united in their office both executive and revenue functions, collected these funds executively in the traditional way and spent them to meet a number of local needs."[5] Gradually provisions were made to levy taxes on the rural people for construction of roads, work of sanitation, irrigation, education etc.

Lord Mayo set up rural boards under the scheme of decentralisation in 1870 with a view to administer local funds. The main objective of Lord Mayo's scheme was to relieve the Imperial finances of the management of local needs. The rural boards were set up in the early period on the basis of election where local representatives used to get opportunity to share the management. There was a President and Vice-president of each rural Board. Half of the total strength of the Board were government officials. It were the Presidencies of Madras and Bombay which led the way in respect of public spirit and voluntary service. Lord Ripon extended a new system of finance by transferring from the "provincial" to `local' activity such additional items of receipts and charges as might equalize local and municipal taxation to secure uniform progress in their development throughout the country.[6] It was he who developed the policy of his predecessors in regard to development of local bodies.[7] He also added a political dimension to the erstwhile scheme of financial and administrative decentralisation to promote local development projects. His famous Resolution of 18 May 1882 said that "It is not primarily with a view to improvement in administration that this measure (local self-government) is put forward and approved. It is chiefly desirable as an instrument of political and popular education", which was essential to acquire skill and experience in the management of local affairs by elected members of municipal and local boards.[8] The elective element had existed even before Ripon. But it was only permissive. He made it a rule and enforced it as an instrument for the political education of the elitist `competitions' who were projecting themselves as a potential alternative to the bureaucracy in such fields of administration were being decentralised for political reasons. Thus Lord Ripon's policy of local self-government in India had two objectives. Firstly, the aim was to build a provincially reinforced local fund in order to free imperial finances from local functions such as the maintenance of certain kinds of roads, hospitals, dispensaries, drainage, water supply and sanitation, vaccination, education (chiefly primary), pounds and feries, markets, rest houses and other minor public works. Secondly, he wanted to reconstruct local bodies so as to provide additional avenues for educated employment and keep the politically motivated elites engaged in the exercise of a measure of power, influence and authority. In fact, it was open invitation to those social elites who wanted to establish their social status and avail the opportunity to acquire wealth and patronage of the government officials both.

Under the Local Funds Act VI of 1871 the Presidency of Madras was divided into local fund circles. A Rural Board was established in each circle with a President, a Vice-President and three or more members, all of whom had to own land, or carry on business or reside in the circle. The Act which vested a local government with powers of taxation did not introduce any elective principles. It was all permissive where the District Collector exercised all discretionary authorities. The elective principle was first time emphasized by the Government of India

Resolution of 18 May 1882. The size of the official membership was reduced and official interference from within was prohibited with a view to make local bodies more native in nature.

The British Government wanted to do nothing in haste. So it proceeded ahead in this direction on the principle to trial and error. It was well known to the Goernment that the Indian society was heterogeneous in character, and it was very difficult to bring homogencity and uniformity in the local bodies. That is why the government did not allow the local bodies to function independently, and kept them under the control and supervision of local governmental authorities. However, it was laid down that the proportion of government officials appointed to local bodies should be limited, and the necessary control over their proceedings should be from without rather than from within. It was Resolved that the Provincial Governments be empowered to maintain and extend throughout the country, in every district where an intelligent non-official agency could be found, a network of local boards, to be charged with definite duties and entrusted with definite funds. It was also decided that area for a local body should not be too large. The Government had already gained experience that local self-government in India could not be practised covering large area due to lack of proper education. So the Resolution of 18 May, 1882 determined to create smaller units of sub-divisional and taluka boards and emphasized the importance of political and popular education to widen the basis of elitist loyalty for the attainment of both local and imperial ends.

Madras Act of 1884 introduced a three-tier system. At the bottom was the Union Board, in the middle was the Taluka Board and at the top was the District Board. The Union Board was the group of villages under the control of a Panchayat, comprising not less than five members among whom one must be the village headman. It may be noted that the Local Boards Act of 1844 had raised the position of the village headman providing the establishment of Union Panchayats to handle village sanitation, the repairs of roads, tanks and walls, the construction of dispensaries and hospitals and the diffusion of elementary education. These functions earlier were done by the village community which were transferred to the Unions now. This was being done by an external official agency as a gift of government, not as something which had legitimately belonged to it as of right. The Taluka Board consisted of a President and not less than twelve members. Out of total membership two thirds of the members were to be non-official. The District Board consisted of a President and not less than twenty four members. Three-fourths members of the District Board must be non-officials. In both the cases the President appointed was an officer of the Government. The Collector used to be the President of the District Board while the sub-divisional Officer was appointed as the President of the Taluka Board. Though there was provisions for election of the Presidents and Vice-Presidents, nomination continued for several years. There was also provision under the Act for District Fund and the District Officer was authorised to levy taxes. No Board, however, was to enforce taxation except with the approval of the higher Government. Like Madras provisions for local bodies were made in other Provinces also which lacked complete uniformity.

The voluntary associations or committees in Bombay received legal sanctions under Act III of 1869 which created a local fund committee in each Taluka providing a two-tier legal system of local bodies. There was no elective provision in the beginning. The Committee was to consist of eight members with the Collector as ex-officio President and at least half of the members being non-officials. They all were nominated by the Government. The Taluka Sub-Committee assisted the District Committee with advice and look after the affairs of the Taluka.

In Bengal the Board Cess Act passed in 1871 was the first legal step towards establishment of local bodies. It established Road Cess Committees with permissive provisions for elective membership and a non-official majority. These Committees were replaced in 1885 by passing the Bengal Local Board Act of 1885. This Act provided for establishment of three-tier local bodies like Madras which have already been mentioned above.

Acts were passed in 1883 in Uttar Pradesh and Punjab to

liberalise the functioning of local bodies under Lord Ripon's Plan of 1882. In case of Bombay two-tier system was introduced in both the areas with certain modifications to replace the statutory local committees established in 1871 to legalize local funds earlier collected executively.

A survey and analysis of the functioning of the Local Self-Government in India during the British period before 1919 brings the fact to the light that despite the provisions for the non-officials to participate in the managements, the government officials had majority and they also had supreme command and influence. In the case of Bengal, according to the Bengal Report of 1891-92, there were as before 30 District Boards and 106 Local Boards and that "all the District Boards were presided over by an official Chairman, who is the Magistrate of the District."[9] The elected members were in minority. At the close of 1891-92 of the 790 members in the 38 districts of Bengal 168 were ex-officio members, 313 were nominated by the Government and 309 elected by the Local Boards. Again of the total, there were 593 Indians and remaining 197 members were either Europeans or Eurasians. In the Local Boards, of the 1,248 members 40 were ex-offico, 739 nominated by the Government and only 469 elected. There were 154 official seats as against 1904 non-official and the number of Europeans and Eurasians was 105.[10]

A question may be raised here as to why the institutions of the Local self-Government remained dominated by the Government while they should have been locally dominated by the local people, answer is given below. As it has already been stated that the British Government did not want to take extra financial burden for local development. So the steps were taken to create local institutions to raise local funds and manage local affairs. It was the question of finance, and Government did not want to rely upon the local members. So the Government Officials got commanding position. Secondly, there was proper lacking of education among the people. Due to educational backwardness there was lacking of political consciousness among the people. There was no sense of political participation. Those who belonged to the higher strata of the society were the followers of the British rule to obtain prestige and status in the society. That is why despite the or participation in the local bodies, their voice remained slow and behaviours remained mild imitating. Of the 790 members in the District Boards of Bengal in 1891-92, 31.5 per cent were Government servants, 28.9 Zamindars and Talukdars and 26.6 Legal Practitioners. In the Local Boards 47.7 per cent were Zamindars, Talukdars or their servants. It shows that most of the non-officials were Zamindars or their agents who did not want to go against the British because their interests were safe so long as they had the British patronage and favour. They thought their participation in the local self-government as a favour done to them by the government. B.B. Misra has rightly observed that the Zamindars and the legal practitioners together constituted the majority in all districts. They could have carried reform and rural financing, but instead obstructed progress in both. The Zamindars who dominated rural areas in Bihar became a united opposition of all land-owners against the introduction of the cadastral survey, a measure designed to improve agricultural production by an attempt to ensure the security of various occupancy and tenancy right."[11]

Analysis of the functioning of the Local Self-Government in India before 1919 brings another fact to the light that it failed to achieve the required purposes. No doubt, the Government got the credit for giving foundation of the local self-Government in India on western style mixing some old Indian principles in Village Panchayats. It is also a fact that the Government made a beginning in decentralising the political powers and giving opportunity to the local people to take active part in local administrative affairs. But the objectives which were to be achieved in regard to local development could not be achieved. Though some progress was made in field of agriculture and tenancy, no remarkable works were done for the rural development. The problem of education, sanitation, water supply, drainage system, construction of roads etc. remained as they were. The factors which were responsible for either failure or low progress of developmental administration in the rural areas are mentioned below.

Firstly, the creation of local self-governments in the districts were not the result of natural growth. Rather it was a gift given by the Government to the people. That is why people remained to the local self-government. Secondly, in absence of proper education and mass awareness there was no public control on the functioning of the local bodies. There existed a little or no organised public opinion that might serve as a check on both elitist and bureaucratic elements in the local bodies. Thirdly the excessive control of the local Government Officers over the functioning of the local bodies was also one of the factors which hampered the progress of the local self-governing institutions in the rural areas. The executive officers had the instructions to watch the proceedings of local boards and point out to them matters calling for consideration. They were to draw attention to 'check by official remonstrance' any attempt to exceed proper functional limits or to act illegally 'in an arbitrary or unreasonable manner."[12] No doubt there was instructions to the local executive officers to avoid bureaucratic despotism, but the authoritarian character of the Indian society and imperial consideration left no room for any relaxation of official dominance. It continued in spite of Ripon's remonstrance against a rigid bureaucracy, indifferent or hostile to democratic decentralisation. As a result, the local bodies remained as instruments in the hands of the executive officers to build the rural India on the line which they preferred. Fourthly, the Indian members of the local bodies had no or little interest in the functioning or objectives of the local bodies. The annual reports on administration in Bengal made it clear that in several districts the Indian members of local bodies took little or no interest in attending the meetings of the local bodies. As a result meeting has to be adjourned on several occasions due to lack of even quorum. It was reported that "These Boards, these of Dhanbad and the Northern and Southern Zamindaries, Sambalpur, held only two meetings each, and out of 78 Local Boards, 32 failed to met at least once a month. The Lieutenant Governor trusts that the grant of travelling allowance which has been sanctioned, will make it possible for outlying members to attend at meetings more regular and frequently."[13] But sanctioning of grants for travelling allowance, too, could not enable the members to take part in the meetings of the local bodies. Both land-owners and practitioners of law as a class betrayed a general lack of public spirit in the discharge of rural functions vested in local bodies. It was the governmental bureaucracy and the non-official European element of District and Local Boards who imparted to these institutions a corporate character to serve as an agency of rural services.

Thus it is evident that most of the Union Committees or Boards at the Village Level very much weak or lifeless even. Since there was very less income from these units as revenue, there was less expenditure on welfare or developmental schemes.[14] To make the Local Bodies more viable The Bengal Local Self-Government (Amendment) Act-V was passed in 1908 which affected a considerable delegation of powers to Commissioners of Divisions in respect of appointment, removal and resignation of members as well as the election of Chairman of Local Boards. The Act also made certain modifications in laws and by laws of the Boards.

The delegation on powers of Commissioners, however, did not signify any loosening of bureaucratic grip over the local bodies. In addition, powers were taken to levy tools on bridges, and the diversion of the road cess to purposes other than those mentioned in the Cess Act of 1880 was prohibited. The application of the District Fund was at the same time extended in various directions. Under the head of education, for example, contributions did not remain confined to primary education under the control of the District Board. These were permitted to secondary no other schools under private management, and even towards the maintenance of hostels. In respect of medical works, authority was given to District Boards to train and employ compounders, midwives and veterinary practitioners.

The importance of a three-tier system of rural boards thus continued to be recognised as a separate local agency of social services in the rural areas. The Bengal Local Self-Government Act-V of 1908 provided for a measure of administrative decentralisation from the provincial secretariat to Divisional Commissioners. It was a step which helped to reduce the arbitrary proceedings of the Collector Chairman and extended the functional scope of District Boards and also brought into focus the projected usefulness of union committees as an instrument of village development. It was within this framework that local bodies functioned until reconstituted in the 1920s under the Government of India Act, 1919.

Some major changes took place in the mode and objectives of the Local Self-Government in India from passing the Government of India Act 1919. As it has already been stated that the newly emerged middle class Indians were not favourable to the legislations done in the favour of rural poor. The middle class Indians wanted to control the legislative machinery of the Government so that they could be able to protect their interests. Hence their demand was Swaraj which the National Congress had adopted in 1906. Now the aim for political decentralisation for rural development began to weaken and the demands for more parliamentary autonomy got force. As a result the British Government, on 20 August, 1917, declared the goal to be "that of increasing association of Indians in every branch of the administration and the general development of self-governing institutions with a view to the progressive realisation of responsible government in India as an integral part of the British Empire." The declaration assured the Indians that the British Parliament would take all the possible steps to give more autonomy to the provincial legislatures.[15]

Thereafter the Montagu-Chelmsford Report was published in 1918 which recommended the grant of some measures of responsibility to popular representatives in the provinces on the basis of four principles:

(a) almost complete popular control over local bodies;

(b) the beginning of some measures of responsible Government in the provinces involving a great deal of legislative, administrative and financial decentralization from the Government of India;

(c) the continuance of the responsibility of the Government of India wholly to Parliament, pending experience of the effect of the changes to be introduced in the provinces; and

(d) the proportionate relaxation of the control of Parliament and the Secretary of State over the Government of India and the Provincial Governments as the foregoing changes took effect." The Government of India Act, 1919 was passed on these principles.

The Act provided for two categories of subjects—the reserved and the transferred. The provincial legislatures got full authority over the transferred subjects while the reserved subjects still remained under the supervision and control of the Central Government. The Revolution of authority to Local Governments was affected under the Devolution Rules made under the Government of India Act, 1919. The list of the Provincial subjects included local self-government, medical administration, and public health. Besides them, education, public works, agriculture, fisheries, revenue administration, forest and famine relief, police, prisons, veterinary, cooperative societies, industries etc. also remained under the provincial authority.[16]

The immediate effect of the decentralisation of power under the provisions of the Government of India Act, 1919 was more democratization of local bodies in India. In the words of Misra the effect of the Act was "attendent influence of national, communal and caste politics that crept into their inner recesses and affected their potency as instruments of rural development on sound administrative principles."[17]

In Madras Local Boards Act of 1920 was passed which prohibited the government officials to be the member of any rural board by virtue of his office. No official except a village headman could contest an election. The non-official Presidents of all Taluk Boards became ex-officio members of District Boards where nomination to the extent of the one-fourth of their total number was sought to be retained to secure the representation of the minorities and women. The remaining three-fourths of the members were to be elected. All Panchayat members were to be elected by rent payers. In 1930, the system of nomination to District Boards was given up, but it was revised in 1934 to give place for minorities, women, Muslims, Christians, Anglo Indians etc. with the result that the problem of rural development which were mainly social and economic came to be treated in terms of politics and the elitist game of power. However, to serve the interest of local development the District Economic Councils were established in 1935 "for the improvement of rural tracts" and these "came into being in almost all the districts."[18] Sufficient aids and grants were given to the local bodies for development.[19]

In Madras the Local bodies were authorised to do several works of public importance and development. These works were road, communications, education, agriculture, public health, vaccination, sanitation, etc. The Local Boards maintained 201 Secondary Schools, 16,893 elementary schools of which 2,760 were for girls only. Though not an integral part of the general administration of the District, Local Boards were functioning as a separate non-official agency of welfare services in rural areas.

In Bombay Presidency provision was made by the Local Boards Act of 1921 for a two-thirds elected majority in most of the District Boards and Taluk Boards. In 1923, the elective principles were further advanced. Provision for direct election to the Boards were made. But separate representation was given to the Muslim community which created communal tension. The District Boards were given authority to appoint their own staff such as Chief Officer, Engineer, Health Officer, and Administrative Officer for education. Steps were taken to ensure economic development like Madras. But rural development suffered in the absence of a cumulative economic policy covering both agriculture and industry. In review of administrative development of Bombay it was reported that an integrated approach to rural development was lacking and steps taken to promote agricultural improvements failed to produce the desired result due to rising costs and the scarcity of agricultural labour.[20]

In Bengal also after 1920 all the District Boards had come under the non-official Chairman. It was all because of dyarchy system of the Government which increased the elective system. There was persistent demand from the Indian Leaders that there should be non-official 'advisory council' to assist the District Collectors in the discharge of their executive duties.[21] After 1919, the District Boards became the agency to advise the Collectors in discharge of their executive functions in the districts. People got the opportunity to meet freely to their elected Chairman. It is evident from the report of the Chairman of the Dacca District Board. The report stated that the people appreciated "the new change of things", which gave them opportunity to "freely miss with the Chairman and inform him about their wants more unreservedly than what they could do to an official Chairman."[22]

The District Boards, now began to function more effectively. The Government, too, became more liberal in giving aids and grants to the Boards with that they performed some essential services in the rural areas. On the failure of crops, they organised relief works. To deal with epidemics, the District Boards made management for Medical Officers in the rural field.[23] A couple of centres were selected by the District Board of the 24-Parganas as an experimental measure and a sum of Rs. 1000/- sanctioned for the purpose in 1920.[24] In the field of education the emphasis of District Boards was generally on Primary Education, including Middle Schools. Their strength kept on incresing, though not their quality. Local Bodies maintained in addition technical and industrial schools to promote rural crafts as carpentry, brass casting, weaving, cane and bamboo work, smithy and fitter's work. They also continued to support scholarship to Veterinary, Weaving, Engineering, Art, Agricultural, Industrial, Medical, Blind and Deaf and Dumb Institutes.[25]

An important change was a shift of emphasis in favour of village unions. The Bengal Village Self-Government Act, 1920 provided for the conversion of union communities into Union Boards invested with powers to raise their own tax resources as corporate bodies. The establishment of Union Boards at the village level was highly appreciated because they did appreciable works in the rural field. Appreciating the works of Union Boards, P.H. Waddell, the District Magistrate of Bakarganj, said that "The time is near at hand when local bodies have much the same freedom as they have in England..." But he was not in favour of giving too much freedom to the Union Boards. He maintained that "England has reached its present stage of development in local self-government after many years and India is only beginning. If control is still necessary in England, it is much more necessary in India for the public benefit."[26]

The Union Boards were invested with certain administrative powers to be exercised subject to the control only of the District Boards. The provisions were made to give more funds to them through the District Boards. All the efforts were applied to ensure that the government officials were not to interfere in the affairs of the local bodies.

The local bodies became subject to the influence of politics and communalism. With the removal of official intereference there emerged a tendency on the part of local bodies to make appointments on communal grounds only, irrespective of the merits of candidates. This encouraged corruption due to slack supervision and reluctance to punish defaultors who might be of the same caste or creed as the majority of the Executive Council.

The Bihar and Orissa Village Administration Act of 1922 and Bihar and Orissa Local Self-Government (Amendment) Act of 1923 were two measures which intended to improve upon the system introduced after the Reforms of 1919. The first provided for the formation in village Union Boards of exercise, subject to the control of District Boards, certain administrative powers connected with schools, sanitation and other matters. There was also provision for constitution of Village Panchayats with powers to decide certain civil and criminal disputes. The local bodies were based on elective principles and had sufficient authority to deal with local matters. The Second Act prohibited Government Officials to be the members of the District Boards. The Act removed all district officers of the Government and made it impossible for its employees to be Chairman or Vice-Chairman even when a Board failed to elect one.

The beginning of 1937 saw the end of the dyarchy system which had effected the democratization of local bodies in varying degree under the Government of India Act, 1919. The new constitution under the Government of India Act, 1935 was founded on the principle of provincial autonomy. Before the general elections held in 1937 it was observed that "the number of district and Municipal Boards with a despite Swarajist majority was substantially reduced."[27] The success of the candidate was mere a result of his own exertions and attainment than the strength and influence of a political party. Consequently, the practical work of the administration received more attention and it was relieved from political influence. The relations of most Boards with local officials improved.

When popular ministries took over power under provincial autonomy, a Development Department was established in Bihar under minister who was also incharge of education. Some amount provided to make a beginning "with a Rural Development Scheme" for the entire province of Bihar. The declared goal of this department was "rural uplift work" the basis units·of the whole organisation being village panchayats. It was to be "a five-year plan of economic recovery of the villages."[28]

No doubt, the goal could not be achieved due to failure of the popular Government very soon, but the Government established a principle in regard to rural development. Rural Development came to be recognised for the first time as a centralised local bodies which did not possess the necessary human and material resources. Secondly, the integrated concept of the goal of rural reconstruction and the necessity of planning to achieve that goal were both implicit in the declared policy which led to the establishment of the Development Department in 1937. Thirdly, the administrative arrangement which was sought to be introduced, envisaged a separate hierarchy of its own from the provincial headquarters to the village panchayat level.

Like Bihar, in Uttar Pradesh also Rural Development formed part of a separate official hierarchy annexed to the Department of Development. Each Rural Development Village was to have either a 'Better Living Society' or a 'Gram Sudhar Panchayat' which remained incharge of development activities in the village. Provisions were made for a regular refresher course of training for the entire Rural Development field staff of inspectors and organizers. The functioning of local self-governing institutions remained mostly under the influence of national politics which cared little for the progress or up-keep of the services that in the past had contributed to rural development under official control.

The Village Panchayat System in India began to get prominence under the Rural Development under the Government in districts. Gradually they became more popular and gained freedom from the control of District Boards in both the ways, financially and administratively. A few years before the independence of India the British Government was applying the efforts to establish the Village Panchayats for Rural Development. The Rovlands Committee was putting stress on Union Boards was convenient units of local self-government for Rural Development with special reference to Bengal while the India Office was suggesting the expediency of retaining the Panchayat System as a primary unit for purpose of constitutional reform in the Indian States. It was Sir Atul Chatterjee, a member of the I.C.S., who advised the Government that in view of the vast majority of men and women in India being illiterate, "Village Panchayat or Assembly might be utilized as the primary unit for frenchise purposes." Lord Linlinthgow also believed in the Village Panchayat System. So he, too, advised the government to go for Village Panchayats in the Villages of India. The idea regarding the Rural Development and Village Panchayats got much force after independence of India.

Thus it is clear that the foundation for development administration specially in rural areas was given by the British Government though there was lack of rural spirit to develop the local poor sections of the people. The major cause of insufficiency in the functioning of the local bodies was inherent contradiction between their elective system and the structure of the Indian society. The elective system introduced by the Government of India Act, 1919 was territorial in nature, formal and based on law. The Indian society consisted of mutually exclusive religious and caste groups, tradition-bound and custom-oriented. So a clash between two caused confusion as well as insecurity in those who, because of their social and economic backwardness, could not compete with members of the advanced sections of society. It is true that the provision for separate and communal representation in the election of local bodies was essential to save the position of the minority and suppressed classes, but considerations of ability and honesty did not necessarily go into the choice of candidates for nomination to reserved seats.

The prospect of self-government during the British not only intensified caste and communal awareness but also brought to light the inherent class approach to the conflict of interests between the feudal and the bourgeois elements of society, a new trend resulting from the growth of middle classes in modern times. Dr. Misra has rightly remarked that "Considerations of powers as a means of individual advancement or a limited group of supporters, rather than the promotion of the general public interest, influenced both categories. The gains derived from democracy in local bodies thus generally happened to be more personal than institutional."[29]

Before Independence of the country the Indian leaders have fully realised that India could not get advancement until the steps were taken to advance the rural areas. It was also realised that the rural development could better be done through rural developing agencies. That is why when the Constitution of India was in the making, matter was discussed in detail what and how efforts should be applied to develop the rural society. Finally it was decided to develop the rural India through Village Panchayats and Plannings. Constitutional provisions were made under the Directive Principles of the State Policy where Article 40 speaks about the organisation of the Village Panchayat and endow them with the powers and authority to functional units of self-government.

References

1. B.B. Misra, *District Administration and Rural Development*, (Delhi, 1983), p. 204.
2. B.B. Misra, *The Central Administration of East India Company, 1773-1834*, (Delhi, 1984), p. 435.
3. B.B. Misra, *The Administrative History of India*, op. cit., p. 4.
4. Moral and Material Progress Report, 1881, p. 145.
5. B.B. Misra, *District Administration and Rural Development*, p. 206.
6. Government of India, Finance & Commerce Department Resolution No. 3353 of 30 Sept. 1881 and letters to the Local Government, 10 October, 1881.

   Also see B.B. Mishra, *The Administrative History of India*, Chapter VIII.
7. I.O. MSS, Eur. C. 144/3 p. 122 Ripon to Kimberly, 21 May, 1883.
8. *Ibid.*, para-5.
9. *Report of the Administration of Bengal*, 1891-92, Part-II, p. 95.
10. *Ibid.*, pp. 95-96.
11. B.B. Misra, *District Administration and Rural Development*, p. 211.
12. Decentralisation Committee for the Royal Commission on Decentralisation, Note on Local Boards, pp. 5.
13. Reports from Commissioners of Divisions on the Working of District Boards in Bengal during 1908-09, Statistics of British India, Part-III, pp. 53-54.
14. Reports from Commissioners of Division on the Working of District Boards in Bengal during 1893 (Resolution No. 4294, L.S.G., Calcutta, 3 December, 1895), Para-12.
15. For complete study of British Government Declaration of 20 August, 1917 see B.B. Misra's *The Administrative History of India*, (Delhi), pp. 57-69.
16. B.B. Misra, *Administrative History of India*, p. 121-3. Also see B.B. Misra, *Bureaucracy in India* op. cit., p. 214.
17. B.B. Misra, *District Administration and Rural Development*, op. cit., p. 219.

18. Report of the Administration of the Madras Presidency, 1935-36, p. XII.

19. *Ibid.*, p. 12.

20. Review of the Administration of Presidency of Bombay, 1922-23, pp. 95-96.

21. Resolution No. 4294, L.S.G. dated 3 December, 1895, Para-62.

22. From J.T. Renkin, Commissioner, Dacca Division to Government of Bengal, No. 4847, dated 8 September, 1920, Para-31.

23. Commissioner Presidency Division to Government of Bengal, No. 17, L.S.G. dated 9 August, 1920, Para-18.

24. *Ibid.*

25. Commissioner Presidency Division to Government of Bengal, No. 70, L.S.G., dated 9 August, 1920, Para-17.

26. Commissioner Dacca Division to Government of Bengal, No. 4847, dated 8 September, 1920, Para-31.

27. Bihar and Orissa in 1926-27, *A Report of the Government*, pp. 5 and 32.

28. *Report of the Bihar*, Bihar in 1937-38, pp. 126-27.

29. B.B. Misra, District Administration and Rural Development, p. 270.

3

Adoption of the Government Policies and Administrative Changes for Rural Development

The need for rural development specially the agricultural sector with an objective 'to grow more food' was recognised in India by the British rulers in the nineteenth century. During the World War II, facing the shortage of food supply, the Government became more conscious about increasing 'the food and fodder supplies of India.' As a result, the Government adopted the 'Grow More Food' campaign and recommended detailed programmes of work for it. Thus, there was a shift in the policy of the British Government regarding the promotion of increased food production from ad hoc measures to planned development for a period of minimum three years. In consistence with the new policy of planned development, a new organisational arrangement was needed to be introduced to ensure popular cooperation. It was possible only when the planning for grow more food would have been done from the below level far from the village level to the provincial one. The instructions were soon passed to all the concerned local authorities to help the Government informing plans and programmes for the rural development. Thus the whole idea underlying rural development in terms of food production before Independence of India was based on the principle of planning from below, from the village upwards through the district to the province.

When the leaders of India took over political power from the

British rulers, they followed the same idea and principles or planned development from the village level for the rural development where the village panchayat serves as the basic unit of rural development agency. The post-independent India's planning strategy in regard to the period and the central involvement in the grass-root planning is indebted to the British Planning System which was adopted a couple of years before the transfer of power. After independence, too, there was too much emphasis on the idea to grow more food by developing agricultural system. Thereafter, the Government of Pt. Jawaharlal Nehru borrowed the idea of Block Development System from the United States of America and implemented it in India all over the country. On the basis of the recommendations of the Balvantrai Mehta Committee, the Village Panchayat System was modified and Village Panchayats were integrated with the community development programme and the national extension services.

The constitutional provision was made in favour of the village panchayat system under Article 40 of the Indian Constitution in the Chapter IV which mentions about the Directive Principles of the State Policy. This Article directs all the states of India to "take steps to organise village panchayats and endow them such powers and authority as may be necessary to enable them to function as unit of self-government." Directive Principles are non-justiciable. It means the organisation of village panchayats is totally on the will and conveniences of the State Government. Surprisingly enough, the Draft Constitution did not even mention panchayats. It was Dr. Rajendra Prasad who initially wanted the constitution to begin with village and go up to the Centre.[1] He in fact, wanted decentralized concept of democracy, but the makers of the Indian constitution finally adopted the centralised Parliamentary system on the model of the Government of India Act, 1936. After a great deal of wragling, the idea of Panchayat System was incorporated in the constitution recognising the fact that the Village Panchayats should be an essential form of "local self-government, as schools of democracy, as instruments of village uplift." To central idea behind organising village panchayats as primary units of local administration was based on the fact that until the local communities were not allowed to share power in respect of their own local development, it was impossible to change the basic pattern of the rural India. B.B. Misra is also of the view that "The inclusion of an article (Article 40) in the constitution, however, represented an emphasis and a reminder of both policy objectives and a modus operandi. The idea was that every state should organize village panchayats as primary units of local administration, deriving their authority from local communities and attending to their needs to the maximum extent possible."[2]

The concept of community development programme is based on the view that so long as the community development programme is integrated or closely related to the existing structure of administration at the local, intermediate or national level, it is impossible to develop rural community. Secondly, it was thought that the people of a particular community or area must be given opportunity to manage their own common development affairs directly under the guidance, supervision and financial assistance of the Government. Realisation must come to the people that the community programmes are, in fact, their programmes and they must have conviction to them. So the Government thought to develop such institutions such as Panchayats and cooperatives under plans so that greater number of the people should participate in planning and implementation of its programme. In other words, idea was that "the Government programme with people's participation should be changed over to a people's programme with Government participation."[3]

According to First-Five Year Plan "Community Development is a method, National Extension is the Agency through which the Five Year Plan seeks to initiate a process of transformation of the social and economic life of the village."[4] Community Development is also known as "a movement designed to promote better living for the whole community with the active participation and on the initiative of the community."[5] The United Nations Report also interprets the Community Development as process by which the efforts of the people themselves are united with those of governmental authorities to improve the economic, social and cultural conditions of communities into the life of the nation and to enable them to contribute fully to national progress."[6]

Thus it is quite obvious that Community Development which is the universal term stands for the all round development of the communities where both the local people and the government participate jointly in making plans and implementing them with a view to developing living standard and taking the due benefit of decentralised democratic principles and values. In fact, a country like India where majority of the people live in the village, and their socio-economic development had been remained in the most deteriorated conditions, requires the efforts to stimulate the vast untepped economic resources. Any experiments were carried out to develop the rural economy even during the British period, but the success was not satisfactory. It was after the independence that the planners of India paid due attention to the local problems in the hope to generate, mobilize and harness the most under-developed national resources.

The objectives behind organising the Community Development Programme was "considerable increase in agricultural production and more specially, production of food grains and development of village and small scale industries."[7] Even from the British period India was never self-sufficient in production of foodgrains. It is true that India is a land of agriculture, but due to poor agricultural management and poor economic conditions of the Indian farmers, and also due to lack of proper technical skill in this regard self-sufficiency could not be achieved in production of foodgrains. On the other hand, there was increase in population which required more foodgrain. It also caused the problem of unemployment. So the Planning Commission of India fixed the target to develop the human and material resources of the area with the people's cooperation. It was suggested that the Government must take active interest in providing technical advise, supplying needs for better cultivation and granting loans to the farmers. So the Government first time felt a sense of urgency to introduce a nation-wide Community Development Programme to bring about rural development.[8] The main objectives to be achieved through Community Development Programmes were:

(i) Area development with a minimum all-round progress;

(ii) Self-help programme; and

(iii) Development of the whole community with special emphasis to give preference to the weaker and upper privileged sections for self-development.[9]

As stated in the preceding chapter, the government introduced certain projects and schemes for rural development keeping in view the programme of "Grow More Food". While giving effect to these projects and schemes the government obtained the experience that the various aspects of rural life were inter-related and that no lasting result could be achieved if these were sought to be handled in isolation. So the community development works were brought under the Community Project Administration to give them integrated character. The Community Project Administration was linked with Community Development Programme which formed part of the Technical Co-operation Programme Agreement of the Government of India with the United States of America on January 5, 1952.[10] The Agreement provided that the programme should in the beginning be confined to approximately 55 projects, each embracing nearly 300 villages with population about 200,000 people. A project area was to be divided into three development blocks, each comprising 100 villages and a population of about 65,000 people. It was decided that the proposed projects should mainly have concern with the rural development helping irrigation, fertilizer application, agricultural extension, health measures and rural education. According to the agreement six of the 55 projects, however, were to be of the opposite type including, in addition to the foregoing activities, small and medium scale industries, township planning and development. The Agreement contained full details and break-ups of programmes relating to agriculture, communications, education, health training, social welfare, supplementary employment, housing and organisational pattern.[11]

Under the Technical Cooperation Agreement of India and the U.S.A. the US Government provided financial assistance. Now it was upto the Government of India to utilise the money and implement the Community Development Programmes. The Government of India held a good deal of discussions with the State Governments in this regard. There was a general agreement on the issue that efforts must be applied through the First-Five Year Plan to gear up both the industrial and general economic development of the country. It was also decided that the benefits arising from both the industrial and agricultural sectors should reach as large a section of India's population as possible.

With the intention to make use of the assistance provided by the U.S.A. for development of Indian Communities the Government of India came ahead. The Planning Commission of India was asked to lay down broad policies and provide general supervision for the agreed programmes. The responsibility to look after the affairs. The Committee appointed its own administrator who began to act as Head of Department in so far as administration of Community Project was concerned. He was responsible for planning, directing and coordinating the Community Projects throughout the country under the general supervision of the Central Committee. He had to maintain link with all the states in this regard. He was to be assisted by a body of qualified staff in connection to advice, finance, community planning and other connected matters. Under him there was a central organisation called the Community Projects. Administration for carrying out day-to-day works. Upto 31st March 1952 the expenditure in this regard was met from the budget grant of the Planning Commission as directed by the Ministry of Finance.[12]

In August, 1952 the Community Projects Administration was given a separate secretariat of its own. Financial powers, in the meantime were delegated to its Director under a resolution of the Planning Commission which authorized him to create new posts in the subordinate services for a specified period of a year at a time and to sanction miscellaneous recurring expenditure up to Rs. 500/- a year and Rs. 2500/- non-recurring.[13] In addition to these Rs. 5,57,000/- was also sanctioned to enable him to pay the salaries of officers and to meet the cost of establishment etc.[14]

The real growth of the Community Development Programme in India began to take place after the formation of a new Ministry the Ministry of Community Development which came into being in September 1956. The development of the Community Development Programme occurred through phasewise. In the first phase, during the First Five Year Plan, fifteen pilot development projects were sponsored by the Ford Foundation in fifteen states. Under the second phase the Government of India inaugurated fifty five Community Projects on October 2, 1952. The third phase began with launching of a countrywide National Extension Service Programme on October 2, 1953.

Under each of the Ford Foundation Pilot Projects a block was created which consisted of 100 villages containing about 50,000 people. The objective behind establishing block was to development scheme' as well to determine the suitability of the extension method and organisation necessary for a country-wide development programme. For intensive development, the Government of India made a beginning with its stipulated 55 community projects located in certain selected areas. Under each project there were nearly 300 villages with an area of about 450 to 500 square miles and a population of 2.9 lakhs. Each Project was divided into three Blocks which covered all aspects of village life. In fact, this stood totally for village development. The main emphasis, in the beginning, was to provide proper irrigation and help the farmers during the time of draught and flood. This was, in fact, an unique step taken by the Government of India with the help of the United States of America. It opened a new chapter in the history of rural development of the country.

The opening of the Community Projects and Blocks became very much popular within no time. It attracted the attention of the whole nation. There was active participation of the people.

New rays of hope appeared among the rural population. Soon there was pressure upon the Government of India to extend the intensive development programme all over the country for which the Government was not prepared due to lack of finance and trained personnel. Keeping in view the demands from the people to set up more projects and limited financial resources of the country, the planners of India began to think about a less intensive programme which could be accommodated within the available resources. So a new scheme called as 'National Extension Services' was evolved. Under this scheme a co-ordinating officer called as the Block Development Officer was provided for a Block with some limited fund and trained staff. Now the 100 villages were put under the control and supervision of a Block Development Officer covering nearly 50,000 to 80,000 people. Provision was made to support him by Extension Officers representing agriculture, animal husbandry, rural engineering, public health, co-operation, social education, women's and children's programmes as well as rural crafts and industries. Like the Community Development Programme, provisions were made for National Extension Services to have village Level workers who must have passed the high school examination. Provision was made for giving them training in extension methods. In the words of S.K. Dey, the Administrator of the Central Committee, "the National Extension Services was a more diluted version of the Community Development Programme."[15] This scheme was launched on October 2, 1953.

The National Extension Service in India was organised on the basis of the recommendations of the Grow More Food Enquiry Committee which had submitted its report to the Government of India in June, 1952. After examining the economic aspects of village life in great detail and observed that since these aspects were all related, 'no lasting results could be achieved if individual aspects of it were dealt with in isolation. "The Committee further recognised that the cultivators would never readily respond to the government's appeal to grow more food unless the government on its part took the initiative and first helped people meet such "felt needs" as education, public health facilities and regular water supply for irrigational and drinking purposes. Hence the Committee recommended that, like the Community Development Programme, the National Extension Service should be organised to cover all aspects of rural life in the country within a period of seven or eight years. The Committee also worked out the pattern of official and non-official organisations at all levels—state, district, taluka or tehsil and village. It recommended central aid to the establishment of the service in all states of India.[16]

Thus, on the basis of recommendation of the Aforesaid Committee the Government tookup the steps to set up the Block Development Offices at the taluka, tehsil or circle levels with the directions to the concerned officials to establish "the closest contacts with agriculturists and be their friend and guide."[17]

In the beginning, the Ministry of Food and Agriculture wanted to control the Community Development Programme and the National Extension Service. But Pt. Jawaharlal Nehru, the Prime Minister of India viewed that the Community Development Programme would soon be enlarged covering thousands of villages, and it was not possible for single Ministry to control and administer it perfectly. The Planning Commission itself was authorised to function as the Central Committee in this regard with the Prime Minister as the Chairman and the Minister of Food and Agriculture as one of the members. All the 'nation-building ministries were directed to cooperate with the Community Project Administration. The Planning Commission treated Community Development as the method and the Rural Extensions as the agency through which the Five Year Plan would seek to transform the social and economic life of villages.[18]

At the state level, too, the same administrative arrangements were made. The State had its State Development Committee with the Chief Minister as Co-ordinator and Chairman and Ministers of the 'nation-building' departments as members. There was a Development Commissioner working under the Development Committee whose function was to coordinate and give the lead throughout the state. At the District Level the Collector was to function as the Chief Co-ordinator and guide the District

Development Committee which consisted of the District Officials representing the various nation-building or development departments as well as non-officials members belonging to the state legislature and Parliament hailing from the district and also some prominent social workers of the district. There was also a committee at the Block level. During the First Five Year Plan a new set of functionaries was injected known as Block Development Officers. They were recruited from the department of Revenue. The pattern of working was still traditional. That is why they remained pre-occupied largely with the attainment of targets rather than the education of people to help themselves through the agency of rural extension.

Both the Community Development Programme and the National Extension Service soon became very much popular all over the country even during the First Five Year Plan. It was seen that between 1952-55, every year 270 Blocks were set-up and at the end of the First Five Year Plan about 23% of the rural population living in 1,43,000 villages got the opportunities to get benefits from the programme. Seeing the popularity of the Programme and Service, it was essential for the Government to improve the employment methods of the concerned officials and impart them better training so that they could achieve greater success.

Before the establishment of the Community Development Programme there was no any such institution which could train the Block Development Officers, Village Level Workers and Social Education Organisers. Block Development Officers were generally taken from the State Services and they were given simply three weeks of orientation lectures. To serve the purpose three training centres were set up by April, 1954 located at Nilokheri in Punjab, Himayatsagar in Hyderabad and Ranchi in Bihar. The forth centre was set-up at Lucknow later on. The first three were the governmental institutions while the fourth one was run on hundred per cent grants-in-aid given by the government. These institutions conducted five courses in a year. Their capacity per course was not more than 200. So the total number of Block

Development Officers so trained up to the end of December 1957 was said to be 1,811 only.[19]

There were five training centres for social education training by April 1953. Five months training was given and each centre could train maximum of forty trainees at a time. But by January 1955, strength was doubled. Thereafter eight more centres were established at different places by 1957-58.

For the Village Level Workers among whom the Gram Sevaks are the first category of village level workers thirty four Extension Training Centres were established in 1953 by the Ministry of Food and Agriculture. The object was to impart to village level workers a six months' extension training in basic agriculture. Since these centres could not serve the purpose as desired. Basic Agriculture Schools were opened where eighteen months training was given. By December 1957, there existed as many as 78 Basic Agriculture Schools and 63 Extension Training Centres.[20] Besides Gram Sevaks and Village Level Workers each Block was given two Gram Sevikas also.

There were also some group level workers and Extension Officers. Arrangements existed for the training of these officers. Blocks were also given doctors for human as well as animal treatments. As the years rolled down and number of the Community Development Projects and National Extension Service increased, the training institutes also expanded all over the country. Today there are many such institutions which are imparting required training to the concerned personnel.

As stated above the Community Development Programme run under the control and supervision of the Planning Commission. By the end of the First Five Year Plan not only the number of the Projects and Extension Service increased but also the responsibilities of the Planning Commission grew up due to adoption of more and more developmental schemes and projects. As a result it was not possible for it to look after effectiively the rural development agencies. So the need was felt to set-up a new Ministry which could serve the Community Development Programme independently.[21] In pursuance of clause (3) of Article 77 of the Indian Constitution, the President of India, Dr. Rajendra Prasad, issued order on September 18, 1956 which stated that with effect from such date as might be appointed by the Prime Minister a new Ministry to be known as the Ministry of Community Development "shall be constituted" and that "the said Ministry... shall transact the business of the Government of India which is at present transacted in the Community Projects Administration."[22] When the matter was referred to the central cabinet, it resolved that "The activities of the Community Project Administration and the National Extension Service are expanding rapidly and there will be further expansion during the period of the Second Five Year Plan.... Having regard to the growing magnitude and importance of this work (to increase food works), it has been found necessary to place the U.P.A. under a separate Ministry of Community Development."[23]

One of the vital causes of failure of the Community Development Programme was the mounting corruption and falling morality of the people of India as a whole. Before independence of the country there was true devotion to the nation, but after the departure of the British from India the lust for individual economic prosperity, unchecked desire for modern comfortable and luxurious life and temptation for false popularity without sacrifices began to creep into the mind of each conscious Indian citizen with the result that the most of the Government Servants as well as public leaders and village leaders indulged themselves into money making affairs. That is why the finance provided for rural development could not be fully utilized for the purposes.

Ashok Mehta Committee

Observing the declining process of the Community Development the Government of India became worry. So in December 1968 and in April 1969 the Government appointed Consultative Councils to advise the Centre and the States on the problems relating to the functioning of the Community Development. On the suggestions given by them the Government adopted some special schemes for the rural development which shall be discussed in the succeeding chapters. These special programmes, too, did not out much ice in the field of rural development. Towards the end of the Fourth Five Year Plan (1970) and the beginning of the Fifth Five-Year Plan the condition of the Community Development Programme began to deteriorate badly. To save the situation the Government started separate programme administered from the Ministry of Community Development and Cooperation. Thereafter, several programmes were launched to be implemented through the separate agencies. Meanwhile the Government wanted to study the situation specially the causes of the failure of the Community Development Programme and their remedies. To achieve the purpose the Ashok Mehta Committee was established which went into the depth of the problem and submitted its lengthy report in August, 1978.

The Government had appointed the Ashok Mehta Committee to enquire into the deteriorating situation of the Community Development Programme and suggest measures to visualize the Panchayat Raj Institutions. While appointing the Committee the Government made it clear that "The Government accords the highest priority to rural development, so as to increase agricultural production, create employment, eradicate poverty and bring about an all round improvement in the rural economy. The Government considers that the maximum degree of decentralisation, both in planning and implementation, is necessary for the attainment of these objectives. It has accordingly been decided in consultation with the State Governments and Union Territories, to set-up a Committee to enquire into the working of the Panchayat Raj Institutions, and to suggest measures to strengthen them so as to decentralised system of planning and development to be effected."[24] Besides these, it also aimed as to provide rural areas the infrastructure for development.

The Committee submitted its report in 1978 which contained 301 pages covering 132 recommendations. The first three Chapters were devoted to a survey of the antecedents and development of Panchayat Raj. It studied the Panchayat Raj System of India from

1959. It discovered some important reasons for causing declination in the working of the Panchayat Raj Institutions. It thoroughly dissected the existing situation in the rural areas and recommended some measures to chart a future plan of action. Giving much emphasis on decentralization, the Committee expressed its view that "The formulation of structural and the utilisation of financial, administrative and human resources in Panchayat Raj Institutions... be determined on the emerging functional necessity of management of rural development." The Committee introduced a new approach (more decentralisation of power) towards the Panchayat Raj.

In regard to the tier system, the Ashok Mehta Committee favoured 'two-tier' system of Panchayati Raj—The Zila Parishad and the Mandal Panchayat. It wanted decentralization of powers from the state level to the district level. The Committee realised the fact that due to expansion in the scope of rural development and also increased in modern technology in the field of rural development, it was not possible for the Village Panchayat which comprised very small area to make effective plans. So it wanted that the Zila Parishad should be made responsible for plannings and the proposed Mandal Panchayats consisting of a group of the villages, and serving as the second tier, should be made responsible for implementation of the plans. It was suggested that a Mandal Panchayat should consists of a population of 15,000 to 20,000. It believed that "A Mandal Panchayat. . . . would alone be able to ensure a balance between technological requirements and possibilities of popular participation in decision-making."[25]

The recommendation of the Committee raised many eye-brows from different corners. Opinion was expressed that "In Ashok Mehta two-tier structure of Zila Parishad and Mandal Panchayats, the Gram Panchayats and village as a unit are casusalities. Villagers come in contact with Gram Panchayat directly, therefore, making it more effective and useful should have been attempted. Efforts all through have been to strengthen the grassroot level but the present committee has thought it wise to shift the power and focus of activities to clusters of villages or

Mandals. To talk of decentralization of power from the state to the Zila Parishad level but to recommend the shift of power and activity from a village to a cluster of villages appear to be contradictory in spirit."[26] Expressing his view against the recommendation of the Committee which neglected the village as a unit of Planning, Maheshwari said that "The Committee does not recognise a need for an elective participative organism at the level of the village; it is content with village committee (Mandals). Such a view makes the village too conspicious by its absence in the Mehta Scheme of organisation."[27]

The issue whether the politicians should take part in the plannings of rural development or not had been creating too much controvercies soon after dawn of independence. The Mehta Committee in this regard was of the view that the Members of the Parliament and the Members of the Legislative Assemblies of the State should be allowed to take part in the plannings through participating in their respective Zila Parishads. It recommended that for planning purpose a committee of the whole Zilla Parishad should be constituted where the M.Ps and the M.L.A.s should be included as ex-officio members. The report of the Committee reads; "The Committee would, therefore, like to emphasise with all the strength at their command that the access of this entire scheme would depend on continued interest, goodwill and cooperation of all political parties." "It further reads We have reached a stage of political evolution when it would be unrealistic to expect that political parties would keep themselves away from these elections, often they do participate though not openly. This situation needs to be avoided. Their participation would make for a clearer orientation towards programmes and would facilitate healthier linkage with the higher level political processes."[28]

No doubt, the Committee expressed its view in favour of the politicians' participation in the plannings of the rural development, but it did not provide any clear picture about the elections of the village panchayats, and the roles of the political parties. In this regard the Committee said that the State Government should not supersede Panchayati Raj Institutions on partisan grounds and if supersession becomes necessary, the bodies disbanded be replaced by elected one within six months. The State Government should not postpone elections as had happened. To ensure impartial and fair elections for Panchayats, the Committee said that the elections should be conducted by the Chief Election Commissioner, and the State Government should contain provisions for this purpose.

For justice to the people given by the Nayaya Panchayat, it was recommended that there should be a qualified judge who would preside over the meeting of the elected Panches.

Regarding the local level planning, the Committee was in favour of the planning from below level.[29] Considering the technology of plans and requirements of expertise, the Committee suggested that there should be a professionally qualified team at the district level for the preparation of a district plan. It initiated the idea of 'planning cell' at the district level which should consists of an Economist/Statistician, Cartographer/Geographer, Agronomist, Engineer (Irrigation, Civil), Industries Officer (Small and Cottage Industries) and a credit planning officer. This cell was to work in collaboration with all other district level officers who would be under the Zila Parishad. The Mandal Panchayats were to implement all these plans and projects prepared by the Planning Cell. The Committee also covered some other aspects of decentralised planning such as formulation, appraisal, implementation and monitoring of projects.[30]

The Ashok Mehta Committee did not want any sort of undue interference in the affairs of the Panchayati Raj System. It believed that no Rural Development would be possible in India until an exhaustive list of functions to be performed by Panchayat Raj Institutions in all the States are prepared and left to the local people for their implementation under the supervision of the district authorities. It felt that these institutions had to tackle 'location specific programmes'. It thought that the development is a dynamic process, and it cannot be static. So there must be 'periodic adjustments' "to suit the changing requirements." So all the development functions should be placed under the Zila

Parishad. It would be the responsibility of Zila Parishads to prepare the plans and projects, and that of the Mandal Panchayats to implement them with the help of the villagers. The State Government, however, would handle such functions such as agricultural research, medium irrigation project, college and university education etc. The regulatory function would continue to remain with the Collector but in the long run the goal to be pursued was that all regulatory functions should be transferred to local bodies and that the Collector should be under the Zila Parishad.

The Committee was very much anxious about the development of the Schedule Castes and the Scheduled Tribes of India. So it recommended that the representation of the Scheduled Castes and the Scheduled Tribes should be on the basis of their population. It also recommended formation of a social justice committee with a Chairman from the Scheduled Castes or the Scheduled Tribes. For providing protection to the interests of the weaker sections of the society, it suggested for formation of a Committee of the legislature with as far as possible majority representation of M.L.A.s/M.L.C.s belonging to the Scheduled Castes and the Scheduled Tribes which would review the working of the programmes specially meant for the development of the weaker and suppressed sections. This committee would also be responsible for social audit of the funds earmarked for the suppressed classes.

Regarding the staffing pattern for the Panchayati Raj Institutions, the Committee was of the view that all the Government personnel working for the Rural Development should be under the Zila Parishad. There should be four grades of personnel. Class-I and Class-II staff should continue to be the employees of the State Government, but they should work under the Zila Parishad. Class-III and Class-IV employees should be employed by the Zila Parishad. Keeping in view unity of command in administration it was suggested that the staff of the Zila Parishad would work under the administrative control of the Chief Executive Officer who will coordinate and supervise the work of the development staff. The Chief Executive Officer was made responsible for implementing the plans and schemes of the Zila Parishad.

Thus it is obvious that the Ashok Mehta Committee wanted a separate administration for the Panchayati Raj Institutions. This separate administrative arrangements were suggested on the line of decentralization of power. However, the District Collector was still to exercise regulatory and other functions in the proposed system.

Regarding the financial resources, the Committee opined that resources must be met from the local level instead of more funding from the state level. It wanted that the local institutions must have the financial resources of their own. So it wanted that they should have enough authority to impose taxes such as house tax, profession tax, entertainment tax, fair tax etc. It further recommended that the grants released by the State Government for the purpose must be transferred to the Zila Parishad, and administrative expenditure of the salaries and allowances of staff transferred to a Zila Parishad should be born by the Government itself.

The Committee put emphasis on close relationship of the Community Development with voluntary agencies and associations etc. It also put stress on importance of training for officials, elected representatives and combined courses for both the categories.

Planning Process for Rural Development

Planning and Policy making are interrelated. Planning is deciding the advance what to do, how to do, when to do it and who is to do it.[31] Planning, in fact, is that activity which concern itself with proposal for the future with the methods by which these proposals may be achieved.[32] Today when the main cry is economic development, the need of planning has freatly increased specially in the developing countries. In a developing society with a backlog of poverty a government is actively involved in the fight against poverty. One of the methods of achieving economic development and social justice is the system of economic planning. India opted for the system of economic planning for achieving socio-economic welfare of the Community.[33] No doubt, planning process started in India from 1952, but a measure shift was witnessed in the planning process from the Fourth Plan Period (1969-70). The most important shift was in relation to the pattern of devolution of plan funds to the state level. This initiated first stage of decentralization of planning process from the national to the State Level in realistic sense.[34] Since then the State Government had been building their own machinery for planning at the State Level and improving their plan methodology.[35] The next step was to take step to decentralise the planning process at district level. So the Government of India set up a number of Committees to examine the various issues connected with grass root level planning and implementation. Among them special mention is required about the Lantwala Working Group on Block Level Planning, and the Planning Commission's Working Group on District Plan.[36]

It was found that the planning had so far remained purely an arithmetical exercise at the national level with emphasis on heavy industries, major medium irrigation and heavy machinery mostly feeding urban industrial complexes.[37] In the rural areas the main beneficiaries of the development have been relatively more afluent farmers who the resources to buy modern agricultural inputs. So the Fourth-Five Year Plan suggested first time that micro level plans should be formulated to correct such implances between the rich and the poor produced by centralised macro level planning. Thereafter, during the Fifth Five Year Plan period a number of district level plans prepared and implemented without unfortunately making much impact on distributive justice and conditions of the poor.[38]

The Planning Commission, putting much emphasis on the micro planning, circulated a set of model guidelines for formulating district plans. Most of the State Governments started district level plan during the Fifth Plan period.[39] Justification for district level planning was given as under:

1. Planning in order to be effective must be related to local resources and needs;
2. Better use can be made of local resources if planning is done at the micro level;
3. Micro level plan is considered as an effective means of reducing regional disparities and removing absolute poverty at the grass root level by encouraging people participation.[40]

It was realised later on that the planning at the district level, too, was not sufficient to achieve the purpose for the rural development. So the emphasis was put on the block level plan in each state.[41] It was felt that there was a need to reverse both the process of planning and system of administration from top to down to bottom upwards as suggested by the Ashok Mehta Committee and Dantwala Working Group. The Dantwala Working Group which was constituted for preparing guidelines for block level planning, put emphasis on decentralization. The Group expressed the view that the Block Level Planning should not be treated as an isolated exercise. It should be treated as a link in a hierarchy of levels from a cluster of villages below the block level to the district, regional and state level. However, it recognised the block as a unit of planning. The block was considered as a certain community of interests which was sufficiently small in terms of area and population to enable intimate contact and understanding between the planners and the people. It was expected that the block could provide an observation platform in close proximity of the beneficiary group and factors inhibiting the uplift of the weaker sections to ascertain area specific physical and human resources potential, to identify constraints inhibiting socio-economic and technological growth and to expand the area of people's participation and implementation of plans.[42]

Thus it is evident that the Dantwala Committee put too much emphasis on decentralisation of the planning process. The Committee envisaged that the planning team located in the district level would essentially move down to the selected blocks and prepare the block level plans in association with the B.D.O., the Panchayat Samiti, Voluntary Agencies and other concerned at Block Level. Ultimately the Block Level Plans presented by the team would be fitted into the district plan. In other words, it was suggested that rough planning should be done from the bottom and it should be lastly finalised by the technical planning team of the district level. It was believed that the active involvement of Panchayati Raj Institutions in the planning process would provide a better climate for people's participation in the implementation of the plan. It was realised that the benefits of the plans were yet to reach the sections which were the poorest among the poor. That is why the process of planning from the grass-root level was suggested. The main thrust of block level planning considering the view points of the local people, was to speed up the process of decentralisation which might accelerate the development process and make planning more responsive to the needs of the weaker sections.

Working of the Community Development Programme

It is true that the Community Development Programme was initiated in India with a high hope of removing disparities from the Indian rural society and changing the economic face of the rural society. It was dedicated to raising the standard of living of the rural people, with their consent, participation and initiative. It was a new hope and vision for the rural people. The Government of India, from the inception of the Programme, set-up several Committees, groups etc. with a view to enquiring into the working of the Programme and finding out some more viable measures to achieve the required success. It is also true that a particular Ministry, namely, the Ministry of Community Development, was installed and sufficient finance was provided to run the Programme. The Programme was designed to create self-help and a sense of participation among the people.

But an observation of the Community Development Programme reveals the fact that the desired results could not be achieved. the programme was launched on the nation level covering millions of villages. It could neither helped improving the living standard of the rural people belonging to the poorest sections not reduced the disparities between the rich and the poor. The reasons which created obstacles on the progress of the Programme are mentioned below.

Firstly, in the beginning, there was confusion about the real objectives of the Community Development Programme. Sometimes importance was given to agricultural production while stress was also laid in developing cooperatives and Panchayati Raj which led overlapping the conflict.[43] So the speed of general people's participation remained very slow and slacking. According to the Balwantrai Mehta study team only 2.5% of rural families had benefitted by the programme.[44] It was also observed that only the small and medium farmers, the backbone of the Indian peasantry class, proved to be dominant influence on public opinion.[45] It were they who got the real benefits.

Secondly, the rural mass of India took the programme as a welfare scheme of the Government which would help them even without their participation. They remained inactive for years. The thought that it was the rural welfare scheme of the Government and there was no need of public participation. It was due to lack of proper publicity among the people by the Gpvernment. So they remained dependent on the government for future development without contributing towards it thereby upsetting the philosophy of self-help.[46]

Thirdly, the Panchayati Raj Institutions through which the Programme was to be implemented remained in the hand or influence of the afluent class who were more conscious about their own progress rather the progress of the poor sections. Moreover, the Government officials and personnel connected with the Programme concentrated more on task orientation rather than process oriented programmes. They very litle interested in the business. Most of them had been put on deputation. They demanded remuneration for extra works.

Fourthly, the Block Headquarters, which were supposed to be the centres all development activities, were not selected judiciously. Most of the earlier programme started by the government were adhoc in nature and time-bound. Further, they were not integrated. Most of the development programmes were often planned and implemented in a fragmented scale and the importance of the totality of the situation was not considered as pre-requisite of development.

Fifthly, no doubt, hundreds of Blocks were created to implement the Community Development Programme, but seeing the size of the country, the number was still less. So these programmes did not cover the whole country. The areas which were brought under the Community Development Schemes got priority for development while the area which was beyond the perview of the schemes remained as it was. As a result, it created regional disparities in development.

Despite the aforesaid shortcomings of the Community Development Programme, it did some notable works and opened the way for the rural development of India which was expanded during the seventies. It is true that it did not cover the entire rural area, but where the Programme was implemented it achieved success, constructing new wells, repairing old wells, providing irrigation facilities to the farmers, and controlling the primary education. Measures were taken to improve the sanitation. Latrines and drains were dug out and drinking water was supplied. Communication system improved by constructing roads, repairing existing ones and metalling some. This brought thousands of villages out of isolation by connecting them with main roads.[47] According to the report of the Ministry of Community Development and Cooperation, in the field of education 7.5 million people were educated. Elwin Committee observed that the Programme was successful enough to be extended.

It is true that the Community Development Programme was a drive of development towards the rural areas. Establishment of the Block Headquarters in the rural areas and recruitment of the staff to work in the rural region was, in fact, a novel idea. By introducing the blocks the government first time entered into the rural areas and established link with the rural people. It not only awakened the rural mass but also encouraged them for participation in the programmes which stood for their benefits. Trained government officials were sent to the rural people to help them in their all round development. Institutions were established to allow the rural masses to take an active part for their own welfare. 'Institutional framework' was first time brought into being for the welfare of the villages. Isolation of the villages which was permanent feature of the rural India, began to disappear though the pace was very slow. In numerous villages health centres were opened and veterinary dispensaries were established. In the non-agricultural sector arts and crafts were taught to the people with facilities for raw material.[48]

The most attractive and important achievement of the Community Development Programme was that it made the Government of India as well as the State Governments more busy to find out some more measures to be adopted for the rural development in the coming years on the one hand, and created consciousness, alertness, enthusiasm, activities and aspiration in the mind of the rural masses for socio-economic development. As the years rolled down, the Government put too much emphasis on the rural development in the plans and initiated some more programmes for rural development which covered many aspects of the rural life.

References

1. Austin Granvills, The Indian Constitution (Oxford University Press, 1972), p. 35.

2. B.B. Misra, District Administration and Rural Development (Delhi, 1983), p. 288.

3. Government of India, Ministry of Community Development, File No. 11/125/58, Administration 1, p. 67.

4. The First Five Year Plan, Planning Commission, Government of India (New Delhi, 1952), p. 223.

5. Cambridge Summer Conference on African Administration, 1948.

6. United Nations Community Development and Economic Development, p. 2.

7. Nehru's message—Summary record of Annual Conference on Community Development held at Mount Abu (Ministry of Community Development, Government of India, New Delhi, 1958), p. 13.

8. First Five Year Plan, Government of India (Delhi), 1952, p. 223.

9. Community Development Panchayat Raj and Co-operation, Publication Division, Government of India, (Delhi, 1964), p. 5.

10. Memorandum No. Community Project Administration/40/52 (November 3, 1952), p. 16.

11. See Appendix-I to Estimates Committee, Thirty-Eighth Report on Ministry of Community Development (CPA), Part-I, pp. 66-69.

12. Memorandum No. CPA/A/40/52 (November 3, 1952), pp. 14-16.

13. File No. CPA/A/36(1), 1952, Government of India, pp. 1-2.

14. File No. CPA/A/40/1952, Government of India, p. 17.

15. Duglas Ensminger, *Rural India in Transition* (March, 1972), p. 6.

16. V.T. Krishnamachari, *National Extension Movement* (Government of India, CPA Series No. 27), pp. 2-7.

17. *Ibid.*, p. 5.

18. Government of India, Ministry of Community Development, File No. F.11/125/58, Adm. 1.

19. See the Government of India, Ministry of Community Development, File No. 11/125/58, Adm. 1, p. 75.

20. *Ibid.*, p. 76.

21. Introduction by S.K. Dey to Ensminger's Rural India in Transition, op. cit., p. 7.

22. MCD/A/85(1)56, (Ministry of Community Development).

23. Ibid.

24. A.L. Pandey, Local Level Planning and Rural Development, (Delhi, 1990), p. 30.

25: S.R. Maheshwari, 'Panchayati Raj between the two Mehtas and

Beyond', *Panchayat Sandesh*, Delhi Vol. 10, No. 10-11, January-February, 1979, pp. 10-12.

26. S.K. Sharma, 'Review of Ashoka Mehta Committee Report on Panchayati Raj Institutions', *Kurukshetra*, New Delhi, Vol. XXVII, No. 3, November 1, 1978, p. 10.

27. S.R. Maheshwari, 'Panchayati Raj between two Mehtas and Beyond', *Panchayati Sandesh*, op. cit., p. 13.

28. G. Ram Reddy, "Panchayati Raj Proposals", Seminar, New Delhi, No. 234, February, 1979, pp. 31-37.

29. Report of the Committee on Panchayati Raj Institutions, Government of India (New Delhi) August, 1978, Chapter-VI (Planning).

30. For detail study see *ibid.*, chapter-VI, (Planning), pp. 68-78.

31. K. Harold, *Essentials of Management* (New Delhi, 1976), p. 53.

32. A. Simon, H. Donald, W. Smithberg and Victor A. Thompson, *Public Administration* (New York, 1970), p. 423.

33. C.P. Bhambhri, *Public Administration in India* (Delhi, 1973) p. 82.

34. Department of Rural Development, Ministry of Agriculture, Report of the Committee to Review the Existing Administration Arrangement for Rural Development and Poverty Alleviation Programmes, December, 1985, p. 24.

35. *Ibid.*

36. *Ibid.*

37. Himachal Pradesh Institute of Public Administration sponsored by Department of Personnel and Training, Ministry of Personnel Training and Public Grievances Pensions, *Course on District and Block Level Planning*, Simla, June, 8-20, 1985, p. 1.

38. *Ibid.*

39. Thimmaiah, G. District Level Planning, in T.K. Lakshman and B.K. Naraun (Ed.), *Rural Development in India—A Multi-Dimentional Analysis* (Bombay, 1984), p. 60.

40. *Ibid.*, p. 59.

41. *Ibid.*

42. Local Level Planning and Rural Development, United Nations, Asians and Pacific Institutes, Bangkok (New Delhi, 1980), p. 225.
43. Dwivedy, S.N., "Community Development Movement", *Kurukshetra*, October 1965, Vol. 14, No. 1, p. 14.
44. Report of the Team for the Study of Community Projects and National Extension Service, Vol. 1, (Committee on Plan Projects, New Delhi, 1957), p. 91.
45. Barbara Ward, *India and the West* (London, 1961), p. 133.
46. Plan Evaluation Organisation, *Seventh Evaluation Report*, 1960, pp. 89-90.
47. Barbara Ward, India and the West (London, 1961), p. 180.
48. U.C. Ghildayal, "Community Development and Rural Growth", *Khadi Gramodyog*, Vol. XIV, No. 5, 1968, p. 398.

4

Integrated Rural Development Programme: A Review

Both the Government and Planning Commission of India had been applying efforts through launching several developmental programmes to improve agricultural sector and the people belonging to the agricultural base. No doubt, the objective behind launching and implementing various Rural Development Programmes was to improve the agricultural products and provide the Indian farmers economic reliefs. These schemes also aimed at making improvement in irrigation system and supplying the Indian farmers new technology and improved quality of seeds and manures. However, the government failed to achieve the desired result, perhaps due to sectoral approach. The poor sections of the society specially the deprived and suppressed people could not be provided with any viable scheme to improve their socio-economic standard. The poor sections of the people such as field workers, wage earners, artisans etc. remained for away from the benefits of the Rural Development Programmes which were being implemented in a fragmented scale and the importance of understanding the totality of the situation was not yet in consideration as pre-requisite of development. This led to regional disparities in the development. It also broadened a gap between the rural rich and the poor. So the importance for multiplicity of programme for Rural Development for general mass through different agencies was lost, and it was realised that there should be a single integrated Rural Programme to be called the 'Integrated Rural Development Programme (IRDP), covering all aspects of the rural life all over the country. Thus the Integrated Rural Development Programme in the form of 'single largest anti-thrust', emerged during the Sixth Five Year Plan (1978-1988).

The Integrated Rural Development is a universal term which has covered all the countries especially the third world nations. Due to prolonged colonial rule established by the Europeans empires, do development could take place in the colonial countries. Their rural and urban areas remained undeveloped for a longer period. India was one of the countries whose economy badly suffered during the British regime. After India's independence its basic problem was how to develop the rural areas which basically constitutes India. To meet the challenge they (governments of newly independent states of the world) began to launch some programmes for Rural Development. Under the integrated development various programmes are put under the single command so that there may be conveniences in implementing the programmes. A World Bank Publication defines Rural Development as "improving living standard of the masses of the low income population residing in the rural areas making process of Rural Development self-sustaining."[1] Bhave defines integrated Rural Development as "integrated development of the areas and the people through optimum development and utilisation of local resources - physical biological and human and bringing necessary institutions, structural and attitudinal changes by delivering a package of services to incompass not only the economic field, but also the establishment of the required social infrastructure and services in the areas of health and nutrition etc."[2] It is a multi-dimensional project which covers many sides of the Rural Development. Since it is based on the integrated approach, it integrates various development programmes. It stands for integration between growth forces and variables, interacting in an over all framework. It is "an organised effort to evolve the possibility of developing infrastructural facilities along with inter-sectoral avenues in an integrated framework at micro level."[3]

Integrated Rural Development is, in fact, a 'package programme of various Rural Development Services and activities of a government which are closely interrelaed."[4] It is also a nationwide movement, stimulated or guided by the government. In this movement main thrust is Rural Development with the help of the rural people who are given direct opportunity to participate in various development programmes and obtain the benefits. These programmes include efficient rural cooperatives land reform measures conducive to cooperative action among farmers, education, family planning, cottage industries, basic technical training for self-employment and many other schemes which help the individual to raise his living standard. According to S.N. Misra integrated rural development programme is an attempt towards the elimination of poverty by providing jobs to the majority of the rural poor and other facilities towards their all round development.[5]

The basic objective of IRDP has been derived from the concept of removing poverty from the rural areas. It is, in fact, a poverty alleviation programme which aims at helping the people who live below the line of poverty to come over it. It does not give any charity to the poor. Rather it enables and encourages them to participate in the poverty alleviation programmes. No doubt, there is provision for loans with considerable amount of subsidy, but it is just to encourage them and provide financial assistance so that they may carryout the self-employment programme such as establishment of Dairy, Poultry, Piggery Farms, Sheep and Goat Rearing, Honey Keeping, Small Scale Industries, Running of Small Shops etc. Second objective of the IRDP is to impart professional training to the rural people so that they may be able to get employment either under the government technical establishment or under the self-created avenues. There are several fields in the rural areas where training can be given to the people for making themselves sufficient. Due to working of machines on large scale in the rural field, need is felt for technical know-how. The technical know-how can not be obtained until training is given. The IRDP stands for providing opportunity to the rural youth for the technical training in the fields of driving vehicles, repairing motors, scholdering metals, blacksmithy, knitting and embroidary, sewing etc. Training in these fields would surely provide employments to those who are in the line of unemployment.

Third objective of the IRDP is to improve the health of the rural people by providing nutritious food specially to children and preganant woman, imparting basic education to the villagers specially illiterate adults, medical facilities, improving sanitation, protecting natural environment, supplying drinking water etc. The greatest hazard to the rural health has been lack of consciousness about the sound health and medical facilities among the rural people. The IRDP aims is not only creating the health consciousness among the rural people but also providing medical facilities among them. It puts emphasis on establishing primary health units in the rural areas, checking up spread of epidemics, controlling death rate of the children and protecting them from vital diseases and creating the feeling and circumstances for small family.

Fourthly, it wants to alter the rural economic face through launching programmes which may help the villagers in constructing roads, approach roads for villages, play grounds for youths, community halls and other facilities. It also wants to arrange rural markets, *melas* (fairs), recreational theatres etc.

Fifthly, the IRDP is more interested in development of agricultural and horticultural products. That is why it emphasises on helping the farmers by supplying them modern scientific agricultural equipments, based quality of seeds, fertilizer on cheap rate, Bazar Samiti for sale of foodgrains and plant protecting medicines.

Sixthly, the aim of the IRDP is to bring about more closeness between the government and the rural people. It wants more decentralization of power and less bureaucratic control in the rural field. The Government wants that the rural development should be through the roles played by the volunteers organisations under the guidance and assistance of the planners and the bureaucrates. The Government also wants to utilize local resources and potentialities for local development. It is possible only when the local people are encouraged to come ahead and help the planners to design the plans for rural development.

Thus it is obvious the IRDP is multi-dimensional in its approach and as a package programme of various rural development services and activities of the government which are closely related with people. It is based on 'decentralized micro-level planning and the block level' and offers a package of programmes for the rural people giving more preference to these who are still below the line of poverty. It is true that before the appearance of IRDP the Rural Development agencies had various programmes for rural upliftment. But they were scattered, disjointed, ununiformal, ununiversal and sectoral. On the other hand, the concept of the IRDP is an attempt to the development of multi-sectoral activities and "integrating the schemes and projects, designed to generate income and employment for those living below the poverty line in a common plan-frame at the block level." "Further it provides a wider approach to integrate sectoral programmrs, area programmes, and rural development programmes in a single framework."[6]

The philosophy of integration of the IRDP is based on the integration of sectoral integration, integration among various programmes and also above all integration between growth forces and variables. Thus the IRDP is an organised effort of the government to "evolve the possibility of developing infrastructural facilities alongwith inter-sectoral avenues in an integrated framework at micro level."[7] Various Rural Development Programmes have been brought together under the IRDP. Now these programmes and schemes are being implemented through a single agency, namely, District Rural Development Agency (DRPA). In the words of Radha Raman Singh IRDP is "an attempt to implement Gandhi's concept of Sarvodaya, i.e. promoting the welfare of each and every individual in the rural areas and at the same time ensuring accelerated development of the neglected and disadvantaged groups of the population with the idea to serve first the poorest of the poor, along with the concept of Sarvodaya in application."[8]

As stated earlier, Mrs. Indira Gandhi, the then Prime Minister of India, was enthusiastically interested in removing poverty from the country by launching some special programmes such as 20 Point Economic Programme, specially for the development of the down and suppressed sections of the people. She had directed the Indian planners and the government both to work for minimising the increasing gap between the rich and the poor.[9] No doubt, almost all the previous plans in India had the objective to remove poverty from the country directly or indirectly. The basic aim of the economic planning of India has remained to achieve a high and substantial rate of growth a progressive improvement in the standard of living of the masses and building up such a self-reliant socialistic economy that there should not be accumulation of wealth in a few hands. From the beginning of the eighties, Mrs. Gandhi began to put more emphasis on making programmes and projects for helping the poor rural masses directly. As a result, the Sixth Five Year Plan (1980-85) resorted to some direct measures for eradicating poverty from India. These measures included National Rural Employment Programme (NRDP) and some other poverty alleviation schemes. The Planning Commission of India once more reiterated its commitment for giving "a practical shape to the nation's collective will for using all the latent resources and energies of the nation for an effective attack on poverty, unemployment and inequality."[10] So the Sixth Five Year Plan sought major employment opportunities in the agriculture, rural development, village and small scale industries, construction, public administration and other services. Continuing the minimum needs programmes, some more measures for Rural Development started under the Fifth Plan, the Sixth Plan, too, searched some more measures for the purpose. While a sum of Rs. 2803 crores was invested in the Draft Fifth Plan for the purpose, the Sixth Plan invested Rs. 5807 crores to achieve the purpose.

It was soon realised that for proper and effective results of development the various rural development programme should be brought under a single Agency for maintain coordination. This was done by introducing the Integrated Rural Development Programme on October 2, 1980. Soon it covered all the 5011 development blocks in the country. The dichotomy between the small farmers agencies and the IRD agencies was done away with. The IRDP included in itself even the Drought Prone Area Programme. The State Governments also immediately set-up the District Rural Development Agencies in each of the district which became the guiding and controlling agencies of all the Rural Development Programmes.

The Sixth Plan of India had put much emphasis on the IRDP and the National Rural Employment Programme with a view to providing employment to under employed workers during the lean agricultural season. It is a programme to give additional employment to the rural workers. Thus it is evident that the government and the planners both were applying the efforts to remove poverty from the rural areas through introducing some poverty-alleviation programmes and encouraging the rural people to participate in them.

Speaking about the need to remove the hurdle of poverty from the path of progress, the Prime Minister, Mrs. Gandhi, while delivering the inaugural speech at National Development Council's Conference held at New Delhi on November 6, 1985, said that "We must involve the people in implementing these programmes. A new life has to be breathed into decentralised institutions."[11] She further said that "No process of development can be socially meaningful, or even viable, if it fails to lighten the burden of poverty. We must provide productive employment to the mass of our people. Development must be accompanied by equity and social justice by removal of social barriers that oppresses the weak. This is the essence of our concept of socialism."[12] Referring her earlier economic development programmes during the eighties, she said that "Our anti-poverty programmes constitute the core of the 20 Point Programme. These will be expanded and restructured to give maximum assistance to families below the poverty line. We have gathered valuable experience to improve them."[13] Thus it is very much obvious that Mrs. Indira Gandhi wanted to increase the scope of poverty alleviation programmes and make them available to greater number of people who, in fact, needed such immediate economic relief.

The ITDP was a novel experiment in the field of Rural Development in India. Its aims, objectives, principles, philosophies and methods of implementation were unique. To understand these qualities of IRDP one must know the specific features of IRDP which are mentioned below:

(i) The IRDP give preference to the poor sections of the society in their all round development. It is an anti-poverty programme. So the main beneficiaries of the programme are small and marginal farmers, rural artisans, tenants, share-croppers, agricultural labourers, Schedule Castes and Scheduled Tribes and like nomands, rural women and children.

(ii) Family is the basic unit of development. The emphasis is not on individual growth but the growth of a family as a whole. The families living below the line of poverty are selected as the main beneficiaries of the programme. During the Sixth Plan a family which earned less than Rs. 3500/- in a year was recognised as below the line of poverty. During the Seventh Plan it was upgraded and a family whose annual income was less than Rs. 4800/- was recognised as a family living below the line of poverty. The Department of Rural Development had issued direction to the concerned authorities that first preference in selecting the poor family as a beneficiary of the programme should be given to those families whose annual income was less than Rs. 3500/-.[14] It was envisaged that about 15 million families were to be covered by the programme during the Sixth Plan, of which 30 per cent had to be from the Scheduled Castes and Scheduled Tribes. Out of 600 families to be helped, 200 families had to be each from the agricultural sector, allied sectors and the industry service and Business Sectors and out of industry service and Business again, 50 families were to be from the Khadi and Village Industries.[15]

(iii) The IRDP is more interested in providing the opportunities of self-employment by providing opportunities for gainful employment and emphasises on improvement in the quality of life.[16] It is also gives special emphasis on labour mobilisation endeavour, where opportunities for employment exists. It is not "a technical but a plan of detailed action for development of the rural masses through providing more avenues and opportunities of self-employment. To achieve the purpose it stresses on increased production both in agriculture and allied sectors, and prefers the role of village and cottage handicrafts and tiny industries. It likes to give primary importance to the tertiary sector for activising the artisans and skilled workers in the rural areas."[17]

(iv) One of the specific features of the IRDP has been that it aims at systematic, scientific and integrated use of all the natural resources available in the rural areas. In the words of B. Rao the IRDP stands for evolving "an operationally integrated strategy for the purpose, on the one hand, of increasing production and productivity in agriculture and allied sectors, based on better use of land, water and sun-light, and on the other, of resource and income development of vulnerable sections of population in all the blocks of country."[18]

(v) The IRDP is based on the grass-root level of planning. This is not a dictation of the Central or State Governments. Rather the planning is made on the basis of micro level where planning experts make the plans with the collaboration of the local leaders, local government officials and the village authorities keeping in view the natural resources and scope and means of implementation of the plans.

(vi) It is not an isolated programme. It is not in a piecemeal or adhoc manner. Rather this programme is permanent in nature and its a part of properly coordinated framework in which the linkage among the different programmes are carefully worked out.

(vii) The IRDP is based on the concept of all round development of the poor rural families. It is not meant just to increase production or national wealth. Its important feature lies in its principle of changing traditional poor rural life and the society both. That is why it emphasises not only on self-sufficient economic life but also a well-maintained modern life where there is a sense of living with at least minimum standard. So it puts emphasis on improvement of environment, provisions for medical care, sanitation, nutrition, recreation etc.

(viii) Last but not the least feature of the IRDP is that it provides for credits to the poor family with sufficient amount of subsidies with a view to enabling it (poor family) to take up and carry on the programme either for self-employment or for time-bound employment obtaining technical skill of training provided for unemployed youths. In the words of Sundaresan. "The IRDP is financed partly by subsidy and partly by bank loan. Depending upon the status of the beneficiaries, either small farmers or marginal farmers, the subsidy varies between 25 and 23 per cent of the cost of the scheme. For Scheduled Tribes beneficiaries, subsidy is provided 50 per cent of the cost of the schemes. The subsidy is provided to make the scheme more viable and to serve as an incentive to the beneficiaries so that they may obtain credit for meeting the past of the cost of the scheme."[19] During the Sixth Plan only there was provision of subsidy of Rs. 1,5000 crores to "male the scheme viable as well as to serve as incentives to the identifies beneficiaries" and the banks were also asked to "provide loans amounting to Rs. 3,000 crores to these beneficiaries by way of credit support under the programme."[20] These loans with subsidies are provided to the identifies families to run the typical schemes alike minor irrigation workers, supply of milch animals, poultry units, sheep units, piggery units, goats, ducks etc. The Schemes under the secondary and tertiary sectors were setting up of poetry units, carpentry units, repairs and maintenance workshops, shoe repairing units, tailoring shops and rickshaw-pulling etc.[21]

Thus it is very much clear that the aims and objectives of the IRDP are vast and multi-traditional. Its features are unique. It covers all aspects of the rural life, rural society and rural well-being.

The Seventh Five Year Plan (1985-90) which was prepared with the objective to eradicate poverty from the country, expressed its aim for "economic betteiment of the poorer sections" by bringing "structural changes, educational development, growth in awareness and changes in outlook, motivation and attitudes."[22] The Plan stated that "The social framework should be such as to provide opportunities for the poorer sections to display initiative and to stand on their legs... such a framework can ensure that the benefits of poverty alleviation programme really reach the poor and are not frittered away through various leakages."[23]

Realising the fact that the qualifying income level of Rs. 3500/- per annum for a family for eligibility for assistance was out of date, the Seventh Plan raised the ceiling upto Rs. 4800/- Secondly, it was conceived that the present level of financial assistance under the programme was much below the actual requirement for bringing the poorest above the line of poverty. Hence it was revised upwardly. During the Sixth Plan the ceiling of 3000 beneficiaries per block was fixed. The Draft of Seventh Plan keeping in view the rapid growth in population, it was too less. Approximately one lakh or even more than this people live in a block where nearly 50 per cent people are below the line of poverty. The Draft of Seventh Plan expressed the view to increase the number of family beneficiaries from 5000 to a minimum of 4500 in the Five Year Period.[24] Regarding the benefit of subsidy its was raised at the rate of Rs. 1,500/- per beneficiary during the Seventh Plan. It was proposed that the total amount required for subsidy would be Rs. 67.5 lakhs per block and the outlay required for all 587 blocks of the state would be Rs. 397.58 crores, out of that the Centre's share was about Rs. 198.78 crores. So with this provision 26.50 lakhs families were to be assisted during the Seventh Five Year Plan.[25]

Putting emphasis on full implementation of the Plan outlays and target, the Deputy Chairman of the Planning Commission, wrote D.O. letter to the Chief Ministers of the states, and Union Territories that "All-out efforts need to be mounted to implement the plan fully and effectively." The letter further stated that "The Prime Minister is... very keen about effective implementation and monitoring of our plan."[26] Thus the Seventh Plan adopted some more vigorous steps to gear up the rural economy and help the poor masses.

As the IRDP is committed to eradicate poverty from rural India by making marked development in production and providing employment to rural masses, the government of India though of creating two components of the IRDP which are the industry service and business (ISB) and the Trading of Rural Youth for Self-employment (TRYSEM). The former scheme was initiated through a government circular dated 20th February 1979 and the latter through another circular dated 20th July, 1979. The circular concerning the ISB addressed to concerned authority of the state, puts emphasis on "promotion and development" of rural industries and rural artisan programme under IRDP in 2000 blocks under DPAP/SFDA/CADP and also in blocks under the Area Planning Scheme for full employment.[27] The circular further stated that the Government of India had approved the inclusion of rural industries programme (RIP) and Rural Artisan Programme (RAP) for implementation in 2000 blocks. So it could be the main duty of the district Industries Centre (DICs) to promote and develop cottage, small scale and tiny industries and small industries and services in the rural areas. They were asked to utilise the available under the IRD for the promotion of industries and other programmes. The DICs were also instructed to make an assessment of the potentialities of the rural industries by making use of available datas in various respects. They were asked to identify and specify the industries/enterprises fit for promotion and development in each block and provide financial as well as material assistance to the identified participants to enable them to set up the units chosen by them. The circular stated that "It is considered very necessary that full advantage should be taken of these provisions for training under the IRDP and training may be imparted in ITIs, polytechnic, training schools run by the Khadi and Village Industry Corporation."[28] It further stated that after completion of training, the trainee may be given assistance upto a maximum of Rs. 5000/- by way of loan from a bank and this may be subsidied to the tune of 33-1/2 per cent subject to a maximum of Rs. 1500/-." Instruction was also given to choose at last 100 family in each block every year for the industries artisans activities. The identified beneficiaries under rural industries programme were to use the financial assistance for buying tools and equipments.

The training of rural youth for self-employment programme, too, to put emphasis on removing poverty from the rural society. It covered in addition to other persons below the poverty line who might not fall in the first category. It concentrated specially on youth. Training preference was given to those who were below the age of 35 years. Moreover, those youths were accepted for obtaining technical training who did not possess any type of technical skill. Here assistance is still given to those who have received technical training under the provision, but in case of IRD persons are identified for assistance often without training. The basic aim of the IRB and TRYSEM was to diversify the rural people to the non-agriculture sector so that the burden on the sector could be reduced and rural workers might avail some extra opportunities of employment. This had been initiated with a sole motive to provide skill and training to rural youths so that after getting skill and infrastructural facilities they may impark upon a career of self-employment. The Central Government decided to, in the beginning, to extend to activities of the IRDP in 5011 blocks of the country with active involvement of officials, common masses, community leads and business houses.

The training of the rural youth for self-employment programme was basically a ruralised economy, and its basic aim was to develop human resource potential in the rural areas.[29] It was an attempt to create a more broad based training system suited to the needs of rural India. It was more informal and flexible training system having less emphasis on paper qualification and other rules, and was considered to be better tuned to the long run requirement of the economy.[30] There was proposal to train about 200000 rural youths in the country every year in various skills. Under this scheme during the year 1979-80 and 1980-81, 93,018 rural youths were trained in various skills and trades like Tailoring, Electrical Fittings, Kasidakari, Welding, Carpet Making, Cycle Repairing etc. According to the government's report out of that 9276 youths had already become self-employed.

During the course of training the trainees were provided with the following financial assistance:

1. Per trainee was given Rs. 100/- per month during the training period. In case the training was conducted in the village of trainee, he was given only a stipened or Rs.50/-. If the training was arranged out of the village, and accommodation was not provided to the trainee, the rate of stipened was increased upto Rs. 150/-. In such cases the rate of daily stipened in courses of less than a month would be upto Rs.4/-.
2. Training expenses upto Rs. 50/- per trainee per month to be given to the trainer.
3. A reward of Rs. 50/- per trainee per month for raw material subject to maximum limit of Rs. 200/- per trainee.
4. A tool-kit was to be provided to the trainee costing not more than Rs. 250/- per trainee.

During the course of training the trainees were helped in preparing project reports which were covered into bankable schemes. They were also helped to apply for bank loans and subsidies. In case of general training the maximum amount of subsidy was Rs. 3000/- while for the training belonging to the Scheduled Castes and Scheduled Tribes the amount of subsidy was maximum Rs. 5000/-. The Central and the State Governments shared the amount to be spent on training fifty-fifty.

An important component of the TRYSEM scheme was its provision for a strengthening of existing training infrastructure such as construction of hostels and dormitories, class-rooms and workshop accommodation, training equipment and aids etc. The government sanctioned a good deal of amount for this purpose.[32] It is interesting to note that numerous rural youths have got the opportunities for obtaining training. Many of them have obtained self-employment also. But there are still crores of rural youths who remained deprived of such facilities either due to their ignorance or due to their non-accession to the authorities who dealt with such scheme.

The District Rural Development Agency was made fully responsible for controlling and guiding the rural development activities. Blocks were adopted as the basis units of planning and implementation of various programmes. Special staff was also recruited to give practical shape to the policies in regard to change the economic face of rural India.

In the early stage under the ISB there was target of one hundred beneficiaries per block per year. Now the target has been raised to the six hundred beneficiaries (families) under each block per year. Under TRYSEM in the beginning, the government had decided to train hundred youths per block per year. Now there is increase in this programme, too. This limit has been relaxed and any number of youth eager to acquire skill can be selected for training. The cost of TRAINING is met by both the Centre and State Governments on 50-50 matching share basis.

It may be noted here that in 1981 the Ministry of Rural Development had set-up a Council for Advancement of Rural Technology (CART) which acted as central rural point for development and transmission of appropriate technology for the secondary and tertiary sectors in the rural areas. In addition to it, the Khadi and Village Industry Sector has also been accorded importance. It had been proposed that in each development block fifty ISB families would be covered under Khadi and Village Industry Programmes every year.

Thus it is very much clear that the government during the regime of Mrs. Indira Gandhi and also of Rajeev Gandhi was highly interested in rural development. The government took up maximum possible schemes and plans to improve the economic lot of the rural poor. Both the ISB and the TRYSEM programmes were meant for those families which were in reality under poverty due to either lack of employment opportunities or due to want of technical skills. But the vital problem before the government was how to implement such programme effectively. Specially selection of the beneficiaries was a great problem. There were many vested interests who were always active and smart enough to usurp the benefits of the programmes. There was attraction for credit facilities on cheap rate and subsidy on the credit which attracted the wealthy persons to take undue advantage of the provisions. A.K. Pandey has rightly observed that the families below the poverty line will have to be listed under different income groups starting from the lowest.... Priority in selection will have to be accorded to the poorest of the families..." but selection of the beneficiaries was in the hands of the concerned staff of the blocks who hardly remained sincerely while performing their duties.[33]

Second problem was selection of the field for industries in the rural areas. These type of industries should have been fruitful and there should be scope for more production and markets for sale of the production. There should also be scope for gainful employment. The participants should have been supplied with requied equipments, skill, guidance, inputs etc. It had been observed that there was several participants who came ahead for installing industries neither for employment nor for production, but for obtaining loan from the banks or from the concerned agencies expecting the gain of subsidies. The government had, in fact, observed such temptation of the vested interests. The government had suggested that while selecting areas for installation of industries in the rural areas, the scope for employment and markets for sales must be kept in mind. So the government had emphasised on need for adequate and proper planning of industrial development and the rural areas.

There was emphasis on the fact that the datas should be collected from the village level by using the village Level Workers. Further, in order to identify industries and enterprises fit for promotion and development in each block, the accent would have to be on the assessment of local demands and resources. The guidelines provided by the Ministry of Rural Reconstructions mentioned that agencies which provided a package of services to a single industry or a group of related industries were more successful than multiproduct organisations. So main emphasis had to be on the setting up or strengthening of such cooperatives, corporation or boards at the state and district level. The guidelines also suggest to set-up Rural Marketing and Service Centre or Village Industry Marketing Organisations. These should have been serving agencies. The Rural Marketing and Serving Centres could be set-up by state level boards and corporations or through the All India bodies in the decentralised sector.

According to the report of the Council for Advancement of People's Action and Rural Technology, one of the weaknesses of the IRDP has been weak marketing strategy and inadequate linkage for the products of the beneficiaries of anti-poverty programmes.[34] Keeping in view the aforesaid facts, a Marketing Division was set-up to be manned by experts. Its basic function was to draw up strategy on marketing and creation of links between groups of rural producers and marketing outlets. The Division would provide consultancy and advice not only to voluntary organisations but also to various IRDP groups set-up through District Rural Development Agencies.[35] The Council for Advancement of People's Action and Rural Technology has sanctioned thousands of schemes. In 1988-89 only it sanctioned 1072 projects involving a total assistance of Rs. 82.02 crores. In the previous years, the corresponding figures was 549 and Rs. 12.68 crores. The projects sanctioned by the Council covered various steps of rural life such as Agriculture, Dairy Development, Village Industries, Minor Irrigation, Fodder Production and certain social activities.[36]

The direct attack on eradication of poverty from the rural areas consists of two strategy. Firstly, self-employment schemes and secondly, the wage employment programmes of the National Rural Employment Programme and Rural Landless Employment Guarantee Programme. The NERP came into being in October, 1980 while the RLEGP came into being in 1983. The former appeared with the marked intention to provide supplementary employment to the unemployed and under-employed of the rural masses, generating assets and improving the nutritional level of the poor in the rural areas. The RLEGP was introduced with the similar objectives. A specific feature of this programme as district from NREP, was that it was expected to provide guaranteed employment for a minimum period of 100 days in a year to one member of the landless labour household in the rural areas.

During the Sixth Plan period, these two programmes provided employment of 2034.52 million mandays with an outlay of Rs. 2,750 crores. Despite these macro-level achievement, the Sixth Plan ended with a light backlog of unemployment target of 228 millions mandays was fixed. The half-yearly target upto September 1985 was 82 millions mandays which corresponded to 36 per cent of the annual target. The reported employment generating up to September, 1985 stood at over 92 millions mandays which accounted for over 40 per cent of the annual target and exceeded the half-yearly target by 12.3 per cent. Out of the total employment of over 92 millions mandays, employment generated for Scheduled Castes and Scheduled Tribes were 32 million and 15 million mandays respectively.[37]

Allocation of Rs. 230 crores was made as a Central assistance under NREP for the year 1985-86. A quantity of 2.3 lakh Mts. of foodgrains was also allotted for distribution among the workers at the rate of one kg. per manday at subsidised prices. About half lakh tonnes of food grain was utilised.

The Central Committee had approved 320 projects at an estimated cost of Rs. 906 crores for the Sixth Plan period. During the year 1985-86 an amount of Rs. 400 crores was allocated for the programme.[38] The Seventh Five Year Plan envisaged providing employment to all the unemployed in the rural areas. About 45 per cent of the employment generation was expected from the investments in the agricultural sector and the rest from the specific programmes of NREP and RLEGP. According to outlays during the first three years of the Seventh Plan for both the programmes were stepped up and placed around Rs. 1200 crores per annum, which generated about 600 millions mandays of employment each year.

A general survey of the programmes and their implementation under the IRDP and the NREP/RLEGP reveals the truth that the government, no doubt, took up decisive steps to eradicate poverty from the rural areas and provide economic relief to the people concerned. The major thrust was on provision for employment. It is true that these programme provided economic relief to the poor sections of the people to a considerable extent. But reality is that the result which was expected could hardly be achieved. The corruption prevailed from top to bottom in the development blocks and the ignorance of the rural people were vital factors responsible for slow progress. Moreover, the rapidly growing population specially among the poor sections of the people was also responsible for blocking the way of removing poverty from the rural areas. However, these programmes generated new hope among them and encouraged them to fight against poverty with the help of the government's financial and technical assistance.

References

1. Quoted in G. Parthasarthy's "Integrated Rural Development", T. Mathew (ed), *Rural Development in India* (New Delhi, 1981), p. 25.

2. G.P. Bhave, "Institutional Finance and Integrated Rural Development", *Kurukshetra*, Vol. XXIX, No. 20, July, 16-31, 1981, Bombay, p. 5.

3. B.N. Verma and D.P. Singh, *Integrated Rural Development Programme*, (New Delhi, 1991), p. 31.

4. Whang, Dr. In-Jong, "Policy Analysis Development", Asian and Specific Development on Administration Centre (Kualalampur, Malaysia).

5. S.N. Misra and B.N. Verma, "Evolution of Training of Rural Youth for Self-Employment in Rajasthan", *Indian Institute of Public Administration*, (New Delhi, 1978), p. 79.

6. B.N. Verma, and D.P. Singh, Integrated Rural Development Programme, op. cit., p. 30.

7. Ibid., p. 31.

8. Radha Raman Singh & Ravindra Narayan, "IRDP and Revitalisation of Rural Scene in India", *Khadi Gramodyog*, Vol. XXXI, No. 4, January 1985, Bombay, p. 177.

9. Chandrika Singh, *Socialism in India*, (New Delhi, 1986), pp. 91-93.

10. Planning Commission, The Government of India, *Sixth Five Year Plan (1980-85)*, (New Delhi, 1981), p. 32.

11. *Gramin Vikas News Letter*, Vol. 1, No. II, November, 1985, Department of Rural Development, Ministry of Agriculture, Government of India (Delhi, 1985), pp. 2-3.

12. Ibid., p. 2.

13. Ibid.

14. Gramin Vikas News Letters, Vol. 2, No. 2, February, 1986, op. cit., p. 2.

15. Agrawal Lata "IRDP and the Poor: A Critical Assessment of a New Relationship", *Coordinator*, Vol. XXII, No. 6, Sept., 15, 1984, p. 158.

16. S.K. Sharma, and S.L. Malhotra, Integrated Rural Development Approach Strategy and Perspectives, (New Delhi, 1977), p. 77.

17. Radha Raman and Ravindra Narayan, "IRDP and Revitalisation of Rural Science in India", Khadi Gramodyog, Vol. XXXI, No. 4, January, 1985, pp. 177-78.

18. B. Rao, Sambasiva, "Sixth Plan and Work of Rural Development", *Kurukshetra*, Vol. 31, No. 3, January 16-31, 1983, (New Delhi), p. 14.

19. D. Sundaresan "Integrated Rural Development Programme", *Khadi Gramodyog*, Vol. XXX, No. 4, January, 1984 (Bombay), p. 171.

20. A.R. Patel, "Poverty Alleviation is a Multi-Level Endeavour", Kurukshtra, Vol. 32, No. 1, October, 1983, (New Delhi), p. 29.

21. "The IRDP Programme", Integrated Rural Development Programme, *National Bank for Agriculture and Rural Development*, September, 1984, (Bombay), p. 4.

22. Planning Commission, Government of India, Seventh Five Year Plan (1985-90), Vol. II, p. 5.

23. Ibid.

24. "Special Programme of Rural Development", Draft Seventh Five Year Plan (1985-90) and Annual Plan, 1985-86, Vol. 1, Government of Bihar, Planning Department, Patna, p. 89.

25. *Ibid.*

26. *Gramin Vikas News Letter,* Vol. 1, No. 11, November 1985, Department of Rural Development, op. cit., p. 4.

27. *Guidelines of Rural Industries Component of IRDP/TYRSEM,* Government of India, Ministry of Rural Reconstruction, December 1979, Annexure-I.

28. *Ibid.*

29. TRYSEM, *Handbook,* Published by Ministry of Rural Development, Government of India, op. cit.

30. *Ibid.*

31. See Ministry of Rural Reconstruction, Government of India, op. cit.

32. Ibid., p. 24.

33. A.K. Pandey, *Local Level Planning and Rural Development*, (Delhi, 1990), p. 79.

34. *Gramin Vikas Newsletter*, Vol. 5, No. 8-9, August-Sept., 1989, Department of Rural Development, Ministry of Agriculture, op. cit., p. 22.

35. *Ibid.*

36. *Ibid.*

37. *Gramin Vikash Newsletter*, Vol. 5, No. 8-9, August-September, 1989, op. cit., p. 18. Also see Ibid., Vol. 1, No. 11, November 1985, op. cit., p. 6.

38. *Gramin Vikas Newsletter*, Vol. 5, No. 8-9, op. cit., p. 18.

5

National Rural Employment Programme and Rural Landless Employment Guarantee Programme: A Survey

In the process of planned development in India, one of the most arduous and vexing tasks has been rural development and upliftment of the rural people from the grip of acute poverty. The Community Development Programme (CDP), National Extension Service (NRS) and Panchayati Raj Systems were introduced with a view to helping the rural masses in their self- development and also emancipate the poor from the clutch of mass poverty. In the different states of the planning modifications were introduced to bring about rural development, and better social justice, but the results were not so much encouraging. The Panchayati Raj System which sole objective was to alter the socio-economic structure of the rural India, could not cut much ice in reducing the gap between the haves and have nots. Rather it enabled the affluent class and politically conscious groups to seize the opportunity for their own development with the result that the people for whom the schemes were chalked out and funds were allotted, remained deprived of the fruits of plannings at various stages. It were the Panchayati Raj Institutions which "protected the vested interests of rich farmers and landowners," and posed serious obstacles to measures intended to alleviate the sufferings of landless labourers, small marginal farmers, as well as the residents of hill and drought prone areas. "To meet the challenge, the Government of

India replaced the Ministry of Community Development by the Ministry of Rural Development on the one hand, and "brought about the direct organisational and major financial involvement in the maintenance of several area-based special programmes and agencies.

Special attention for Rural Development by launching new economic projects and schemes under various agencies keeping in view to enable the rural unemployed people, was paid by Late Mrs. Indira Gandhi, the Prime Minister of India. The thumping victory of Mrs. Gandhi in the mid-term parliamentary elections in 1971 was a turning point in the economic history of India. Before the election she had become very much controversial figure all over the country for her decisive and bold steps for nationalising fourteen big commercial banks and abolishing the practice of Privy Purses in the interests of the Indian Ex-rulers and Ex-princes.[1] She had given slogans like 'Garibi Hatao' and Bekari Hatao' (removing poverty and remove unemployment) during the election.

After the election she appeared as the *Mashiah* of the poor and down trodden section of the people had offered her massive mandate during the election. Now it was her moral responsibility to work for the poor who had mostly lived in the rural areas. Soon after assuming the power, Mrs. Indira Gandhi applied the efforts to bring about conceputal changes in the policy-matter regarding the changes in the socio-economic fields. However, it was no so easy. There were still numerous forces and vested interests who were ready to put obstacles on the way of progressive path of her government. But her determination to work for removal of poverty was firm and hard. She could not bow down before such forces and adopted various policies and programmes to remove poverty from the country and enable the poor families to earn more for better life and living standard. Her government directed the Planning Commission to prepare plans in this respect. From the beginning the Indian planners had put much emphasis on the growth of agriculture. Upto early sixties rural development was synonymous with the concept of agricultural development.

Now Mrs. Gandhi the then Prime Minister of India, took the lead and adopted the policies for drifting the national finance towards the rural areas specially among the poor sentions through different development projects and schemes.

Special attention for rural development by launching new projects and schemes through various agencies began to emerge from 1975. No doubt, the Indian National Congress had been talking a lot for establishment of egalitarian society even before India's independence. The Congress in its various annual conferences had passed several resolutions putting special emphasis on 'socialistic pattern of society' by removing poverty from the country and creating more economic avenues in the interests of the general mass.[2] Under the leadership of Pt. Jawaharlal Nehru the Indian National Congress had laid down the foundation of the socialistic pattern of society, no doubt, but the efforts applied by his government in this direction was not to the mark. However, the Congress under the leadership of Mrs. Gandhi adopted the policies which encouraged the general poor mass. She took up the dynamic lead and her government adopted various programmes to eradicate poverty and provide economic relief specially to the poor families. The government spent huge amount of money over those schemes and projects. In 1975, she had launched 20 Point Economic Programme. It was this programme which was called as 'A New Deal; After her death, her successor and son, late Rajiv Gandhi carried on the programmes launched by her and also launched some more economic programmes keeping in view the interests of the poor. It was 20-Point Economic Programme which had laid down the foundation of the Integrated Rural Development Programme (IRDP). It had put emphasis on reviewing the programme of minimum wages for agricultural labourer and accelerating programmes for development of the Scheduled Castes and Scheduled Tribes. These programmes included welfare of women and children by providing nutritious food to them.

The Fifth Five Year Plan envisaged progressive approach to self-reliance which meant elimination of the explortative forces and divert the finance towards more welfare to the poor sections of the people. The basic aim of the plan was to remove poverty from the country. She had warned the vested interests that "There could be no softness in the war on poverty... There could be no gradual percolation to better living. There should be as a change, but it is so gradual, it takes so much time, it will not be tolerated by any body who is concerned with the poorest or of the poorest sections themselves. It is obvious that there could be some kind of revolution in our thinking and in our action."[3] Thus it is obvious that Mrs. Gandhi was prepared to do something decisively to upgrade the standard of those who were still living below the line of poverty."

The Planning Commission of India was asked to follow the guidelines provided by Mrs. Indira Gandhi and the Commission explicitly declared that "The current level of inequality is incompatible with our goal of removal poverty."[4] It was a clear indication that the government was determined to work for the interest of the poor even at the cost of displeasure of the reactionary forces.

The new pattern of policy of the Government of India under the leadership of Mrs. Indira Gandhi and her successors covered not only the farmers but also the poor people belonging to different professions and living specially in the rural side. In the words of B.P. Maithani "Since the seventies the emphasis shifted from agriculture, and Rural Development was denied as a strategy designed to improve the economic and social life of a specific group of people living below the poverty lines."[5] Now the planners got involved in making plans not only for agricultural development but all aspects of the village economy. During the sixties, there were agricultural production oriented programme like Intensive Agricultural District Programme, Intensive Agricultural Area Programme etc. Soon after changing the concept of rural planning, the new plans were prepared which carried the programmes like Small Farmers Development Agencies, Marginal Farmers and Agricultural Labour Development Agency, Cash Employment Programme for upliftment of the rural people and the Minimum Need Programme. All these programmes were poverty alleviation programmes.

Before the Sixth Five Year Plan the target was to develop agriculture in India. The main objective was to identify the participants, study their problems, draw out suitable programmes for them (farmers of small cadre) and arrange extension service as well as institutional support for the implementation of the programmes.[6] The schemes were centrally sponsored. The main purpose behind launching such programmes was to provide social and economic justice in the rural areas to the poorer sections of the society.[7] This is evident from the statement issued by the Credit Committee which explicitly stated that:

"They had to help identify the special problems of small farmers as producers. To find the means which would make them viable and the methods needed to achieve this. Lastly, to make use of available infrastructure and funds to undertake the needed measures. The agencies also had to see that the extension, input supply agencies and cooperatives provide facilities to the small farmers adequately and timely. The agencies had to give incentives to the credit institutions so that they could give credit to small holders. It also had to make sure of availability of services."[8]

Two agencies—the Small Farmers Development Agency (SFDA) and the Marginal Farmers and Agricultural Labourers Agency (MFAL), worked with marked objectives, no doubt, but it could not achieve the targets due to several factors.[9] In the opinion of S.M. Pandey and J.S. Sodhi the agencies did not perform well and the achievements were not in correspondence with the target fixed. The logic was advanced by the personnel responsible for implementation of the progammes that the target was too large to achieve. Reality is that many of the beneficiaries did not understand the purpose and the value of the agencies. Perhaps their illigeracy was one of the biggest causes of their ignorance about the schemes. The village level workers who were supposed to create awareness among the villagers did not take much trouble to do so. As stated above, during eighties, the government of Mrs. Gandhi with a determination to work for the deprived sections of the people, opened new front for rural development and created a new agency which involved a multi-dimensional effect with special emphasis on the development and conservation of natural resources like alden and water. Now it was not possible for the Ministry of Agriculture and Irrigation to look after properly the work of new projects for Rural Development. Hence a new Department of Rural Development was created in October, 1974. The newly created Department was made responsible for the work of the erstwhile Department of Community Development and also for that relating to agricultural credit and rural indebtedness, including cooperation in the agricultural sector.[10]

The need of Rural Development Department was felt to give more concentration on special programmes for the weaker sections of society as well as credit and marketing facilities. As stated above, the government with the marked determination went ahead to work for welfare and upliftment of the poor sections of the society.

Rural Development, upliftment of the rural people and more specially the alleviation of rural poverty continue to be the central concern of development planning in India. Rural Development is wide concept encompassing all aspects of improvement in the quality of rural life. It implies both economic betterment of the people and effective social transformation. But in its limited interpretation, rural development has come to mean a direct attack on rural poverty through special employment programmes, land reforms, area development programmes and measures to provide safe drinking water supply and rural housing and rural sanitation. Efforts continue to bring down the poverty levels by providing institutional credit and subsidy.

Consistent with the need to step up rural development efforts, particularly in the context of the structural adjustments in the economy, substantial increase has been made in the rural development outlay for the Eighth Five Year Plan. While central sector expenditure was Rs. 10,950 crore in the Seventh Plan, the

Central Plan outlay for Rural Development has been stepped up to Rs. 30,000 crore in the Eighth Five Year Plan. This is exclusive of the likely State Plan Outlay of about Rs. 15,000 crore in the Eighth Plan period.[11]

In his foreword to the Eight Plan it has been observed by the Prime Minister, "Human Development, in all its may facets, is the ultimate goal of the Eighth Plan. It is towards fulfilling this goal that the Eighth Plan accords priority to the generation of adequate employment opportunities to achieve near-full employment by the turn of the century, building up of people's institutions, control of population, eradication of illeteracy, provision of safe drinking water supply and primary health facilities to all, growth and diversification of agriculture to achieve self-sufficiency in food-grains and generate surplus for exports."[12]

The IRDP was a major self-employment programme for the upliftment if rural poor families below the poverty line. Under the IRDP income generation assets were provided to families below the poverty line through a mix of subsidy and credit. Credit linkage is obligatory except Rs. 1000 crore. Both the Governments of India and the states provided subsidy on the ratio of fifty-fifty per cent. The Development of Women and Children in Rural Areas Programme was introduced in 50 Districts in 1982-93 as a Centrally Sponsored Schemes of the Department of Rural Development with UNICEF cooperation to strengthen the women of poor households so as to enable their organised participation in social development towards self-reliance. This programme was supported by the District Rural Development Agency through a team of functionaries supervised by an Assistant Project Officer. The State Government provided resources for management training and cash support to the revolving fund for the women groups.

The training of Rural Youth for Self-Employment is a supporting component of the IRDP. Started as a centrally sponsored scheme on 15th August, 1979, it aims at providing technical and entrepreneurial skills to rural youth from families below the povery line to enable them to take up income generating activities.

The trainees receive stipends during their training and given suitable kits free of cost. Honorarium is also paid to training institutions, masters and craftsman. Payment is made for purchase of raw materials. Financial assistance is provided to training institutions. From 1991-92 recurring expenses have been declined from IRDP and a separate allocation has been provided. From 1991 rate of stipends has also been increased.

The IRDP was a multifacet economic scheme which included several programmes. The National Rural Employment Programme (NREP) and the National Rural Employmented Guarantee Programme (NREGP) are the programmes which were launched under the IRDP with the objective to provide employment those rural families which were still below the line of poverty or the members of such poor families had no opportunity to work all round the year. Rural poverty alleviation has been of primary concern in the economic planning and development process of the country. Rural areas account for nearly three-fourth of the population of the country and have a much larger concentration of people below the poverty line. People living in these areas specially the poor one, were those who could not attain minimum standard of living. Extensive efforts have been made to identify the poor in the country so that the programmes of poverty alleviation and employment generation are better targeted and achieved.

Being a predominantly rural economy, the development of rural areas and rural people, particularly the vulnerable sections amongst them, continued to be the central concern of the development planning in India in the Eighth Plan. It was a message of this concern of the development planning which attracted the attention of a larger section of the poor people all over the country who immediately needed employment. It was a measure of this concern that the Central outlay for Rural Development had been stepped up to Rs. 3000 crore compared to the actual expenditure of Rs. 11,000 crore during the Seventh Plan period and Rs. 2,800 crore in the Sixth Plan.[13] Hence the Eighth Plan played vital role in tackling the rural poverty and laid a solid foundation for the Ninth Plan. It was the Eighth Plan which put emphasis on human development in all its facets as the core of development efforts. The expanded focus on poverty alleviation programme which included NREP and NREGP was aimed at giving employment and income to rural poor through self-employment, wage employment and development of remote and backward areas. The emphasis on employment is important not only from the point of view of poverty alleviation but also for effective utilisation of the vast human resources available in the country for economic and social development. There is also renewed emphasis on making the people active participants in the development process with the government playing an enabling and facilitating role. It is within the framework of these broad objectives of the Eighth Five Year Plan that the annual plans had been formulated.

Programmes on Integrated Rural Development Programme (IRDP), National Rural Employment Programme NREGP) Jawahar Rojgar Yojana (JRY), Accelerated Rural Water Supply Programme, Draught Prone Areas Programme, Desert Development Programme, Training of Rural Youth for Self-Employment (TRYSEM), Development of Women and Children in Rural Areas (DWCRA), Rural Sanitation Programme, Land Reforms, Road in Special Problem Areas, State Institute of Rural Development (SIRD), Extension of Voluntary Schemes, Media and Communication and Agricultural Marketing were under implementation at the beginning of the Eighth Plan.

Mrs. Indira Gandhi, the then Prime Minister of India, speaking about the significance of the programmes for development of the rural areas said in 1975:

"The task before us is to bring about faster and more even agricultural growth... Our anti-poverty programmes constitute the core of the 20-Point Programme. These will be expanded and restructured to give maximum assistance to families below the poverty line. We have gathered valuable experience in implementing these programmes. We must use the experience to improve them. We must involve the people in implementing these programmes. New life has to be breathed into decentralised institutions."[14]

Putting emphasis on the significance of employment in the rural areas for the poor people, she said that "One of our fundamental priorities is expansion of employment. The strategies policies and programmes of the Seventh Plan are geared to this objective. We propose to increase employment faster than the growth of the labour forces."[15] To achieve the objective fixed the Sixth Plan, the Seventh Plan period chalked out schemes for employment in the rural areas through the NREP, NREGP and TRYSEM. This is evident from her instructions given to the states of India. She said that "Now that the plan outlays and targets have been broadly agreed upon, all out efforts need to be mounted to implement the plan fully and effectively. "She further instructed to the State Governments that "The earmarking schemes will have to be enforced more strictly during the seventh plan to ensure better implementation in the priority sectors." The State Governments were provided "opportunity to suggest changes in the earmarking, taking into accounts the effects of any unforeseen developments beyond their control in adhering to the earmarking."[16]

For the year 1985, under the scheme of National Rural Employment Programme, an employment target of 228 million mandays had been fixed. The half-yearly target up to September, 1985 stood at over 92 million mandays which accounted for over 40% of the annual target and exceeded the half-yearly target by 12.3%. For the corresponding period, last year, the reported employment generation was 92.2 million mandays.[17] The achievement of the year 1985 was marginally lower than that of the last year's corresponding period. However, it may be mentioned that the employment target for the year 1985 had been reduced by 26% from last year's target of 309.13 million mandays as a result of escalation in cost of materials and increase in wage rate for the workers employed under the Programme. The actual employment generation was expected higher after successful implementation of the schemes and programmes in the states.

Analysis of employment generation upto September, 1985 indicates that performance in 11 States had been above the national average.[18]

Orissa which had lagged behind the target in the last few years also showed creditable performance. As against last year's employment generation of over 35 lakhs mandays, the current year's achievement was over 56 lakh mandays. The performance in Rajasthan had also been quite impressive. It had recorded about 62 lakh mandays against the target of generating 45 lakh mandays giving a percentage achievement of 138%. Last year's achievement in the State for the corresponding period was only about thirteen and a half lakh mandays.

Out of the total employment generation of over 92 million mandays, employment generation for the Scheduled Castes and Scheduled Tribes were over 32 million and 15 million mandays respectively. The combined employment generation for Scheduled Castes and Scheduled Tribes was 47.6 million mandays which represented 51.7% of the total reported employment generation. Employment generated for landless category had been reported as 23.7 million mandays which accounted for roughly 1/4th of the total reported employment generation.

An allocation of Rs. 230 crores had been provided as Central Assistance under the National Rural Employment Programme (NREP) for the year 1985. As against this Rs. 127.40 crore had been released towards first instalments to the States and the Union Territories which included 20% earmarked allocation of Central share under social forestry. In order to maintain the momentum gathered in implementation of the Programme, first instalment of Central Assistance was released to the States without insisting on the fulfilment of certain stipulated conditions for the release of the Central share. The reported utilisation upto September, 1985 was around Rs. 150 crore giving a percentage utilisation of 33 against the current year's (1985) utilization. Again for the year, a quantity of 2.3 lakh MTs of foodgrains had also been allotted for distribution among the workers at the rate of one kilogram per manday at subsidised prices. About half lakh tonnes of foodgrains had been utilised. In some of the major States like Madhaya Pradesh and Uttar Pradesh, there had been significant improvement in foodgrain utilisation. The provided some more convenient to the village workers. The foodgrains distributed among them were not of high quality, however, that was given on the subsidised rate which gave economic relief to the concern people.

Twenty per cent of the allocation (Rs. 91.50 crore) under the NREP was earmarked for social forestry and the entire earmarked allocation from the Central share had been released along with the first instalment. A decision had been taken to fix targets under social forestry sector and the States had been requested to work out appropriate targets for the year 1985-86 and monitor the progress periodically.[19] Ten per cent of the allocation was earmarked for works directly benefitting Scheduled Castes and Scheduled Tribes. The earmarked allocation for the year 1985-86 was Rs. 45.75 crore.

So far the implementation of the Rural Landless Employment Guarantee Programme (RLEGP) was concern, the Central Committee had approved 320 projects at an estimated cost of over Rs. 906 crore for the Sixth Plan period. The position with regard to submission of the projects and sanction was fairly satisfactory according the report of the government. The spill-over cost of the projects during 1985-86 was over 334 crore. Funds available during the year were Rs. 500 crore including foodgrains subsidy.[20] New projects to the extent of Rs. 396 crore were earmarked for the year 1985 only. Since 20% of the funds had been earmarked for social forestry and States had been permitted to commence implementation of social forestry projected in anticipation of Central Committee's approval, a further Rs. 92.70 crores social forestry projects were under implementation.

During the year 1985-86, an amount of Rs. 400 crore (including foodgrains subsidy etc.) had been allocated for the programme. Against this Rs. 253.23 crore had been released to the

States and Union Territories as first instalment which also included the earmarked funds for social forestry projects.[21]

The expenditure reported during the first quarter of the year 1985-86 was Rs. 130.80 crore which represented 33.71% of the allocation and 25.82% of the availability of funds under the Programme (excluding Rs. 100 crore meant for the Scheduled Castes and Scheduled Tribes). There had been considerable increase in expenditure during the quarter ending September, 1985 as compared with the previous quarter and also over the corresponding quarter of the last year and 16.89% over the previous quarter. The State Governments of Assam, Bihar, Gujarat, Haryana, Kerala, Maharashtra, Meghalaya, Nagaland, Orissa, Sikkim, Tripura and West Bengal had far exceeded the expenditure during the quarter.

Employment generation is of the order of slightly above 900 lakh mandays which was 119% of the six monthly target of about 756 lakh mandays and 43% of the annual target of about 2098 lakh mandays. The states which had performed better than the national level were Assam, Gujarat, Himachal Pradesh, Maharashtra, Nagaland, Punjab, Rajasthan and West Bengal. It had also been seen that employment generation during the quarter ending September, 1985 was higher by 34.44 per cent than the previous quarter and higher by about 68% of the employment generated during the corresponding quarter of the last year. The states which had reported higher employment generation during the quarter of the last year were Assam, Bihar, Gujarat, Haryana, Himachal Pradesh, Orissa, Rajasthan, Tripura, Uttar Pradesh and West Bengal. In employment generation the performance was ahead by more than two months as the reported employment generation of about 900 lakh mandays was higher than the employment generated upto November last year which was about 806 lakh mandays only. Since the reports received so far were incomplete, the position of the employment generation could be much better that what was available then.

The break-up of employment generation in terms of the Scheduled Castes and Scheduled Tribes was available for about

726 lakh mandays. Employment which was 27.27% and to those of Scheduled Tribes was about 127 lakh mandays which was 17.54%. Thus a total of about 45% of employment had been provided to the Scheduled Castes and the Scheduled Tribes. The employment provided to the landless was about 359 lakh mandays which was about 42%.[22]

So far the distribution of foodgrains among the poor working class was concerned, the year 1985-86 produced a record. A quantity of 1,45321 MTs was released for first and second quarter of the year. This included the additional food grains released to the State Governments of Bihar, Gujarat, Madhya Pradesh and Uttar Pradesh.[23]

The reported utilisation of foodgrains was 42,931 MTs which was 29.44% of the released and 20.44% of the allocations of 2,10,000 MTs. However, there had been considerable increase in the utilisation of foodgrains during the year 1985-86 as compared to the utilisation of foodgrains during the corresponding period of the last year. The utilisation of foodgrains upto September, 1985 was higher than the utilisation upto November during the last year. Moreover the reports were incomplete and hence the position regarding utilisation of foodgrains could be much better than the one available now.

The Central Committee at its meeting held on 29th August, 1985, reviewed the performance of the Programmes and also reviewed the progress made by the State Governments of Manipur, Meghalaya, Nagaland, and Tripura. In addition to this the areas officers also undertook visits to State and Union Territories for monitoring the Programme during the quarter ending September, 1985. The results of implementation of the Programme were found satisfactory. In its assessment of the implementation of the 20-Point Programme, the Planning Commission had rated the performance of NERP and RLEGP during the first two quarters of the current financial year (1985) as very good.[24]

An observation of the functioning of the NREP and RLEGP and their results brings the fact to the light that these Programmes were launched with great enthusiasm and expectation that the poverty people would be benefited much. However, the results are not much encouraging due to faculty implementation of Programmes all over the country. The beneficiaries remained deprived of actual benefits due to several factors. Due to prevalence of mass corruption among the government officials and also due to their non-commitment to the programmes the programmes could not be implemented in the right direction. No doubt, the Programme provided too much economic relief to the poor family by providing them some additional works. But keeping in view the number of the poor families or unemployed rural mass, the jobs provided were insufficient and part-time. Despite a number of projects and schemes under the NREP and RLEGP poverty could hardly been removed from India. Mass prevalent corruption among the government servants and mass illiteracy among the rural people have remained greatest hurdles to implement any programme of poverty alleviation in India. Huge amount of money was spent, no doubt, but it is a fact that these funds were pocketed by vested interests to enrich themselves. We a result, the gap between the rich and the poor in India has increased. The Indian society is not yet free from poverty and exploitative elements. V.M. Dandekar and Nilkanth Rath, while examining how the benefits of development programmes were shared between different sections of population, came to the conclusion that the process of development in the rural section "has benefited the upper middle and the rich section much more than the middle, the lower middle and poorer sections."[25] The Sixth Planning Commission also accepted that around 50% of the population of India lived below the poverty line facing a number of difficulties and inconveniences.[26] This shows that the programmes and policies of the Government of India have remained helpful no doubt, but results are discouraging.

References

1. Fourteen major commercial banks of India were nationalised by the government of Mrs. Gandhi in July 19, 1969 by promulgating an Ordinance. There was an Ordinance issued in September, 1970 to abolish the payment of pensions and other pre-requisites guaranteed to the previous Indian rulers. These steps of Mrs. Gandhi were taken in the interest of the poor and to serve the cause of socialistic pattern of society in India.

2. Pattabhi Sitaramaya, The History of Indian National Congress - 1885-1935, Vol. I, op. cit., p. 343. Also see, Indian National Congress Resolution on Fundamental Rights and Economic Programmes, the Karachi Session, 1931.

3. Quoted in C. Ganguli's Studies in India's Economic Problem, (Calcutta, 1980), p. 700.

4. Ibid., p. 700.

5. B.P. Maithani, "Organisational Design for Rural Development in North-Eastern Region", Rural Development in North-East India, P.D. Saikia & U. Phukan (Eds). (Delhi, 1989), p. 49.

6. See, Rural Development, Directive of Advertising and Visual Publicity, Ministry of Publicity and Broadcasting, Government of India, (New Delhi), pp. 6-7.

7. R.L. Pitale, "A New Deal Farmers", *Yojana* Vol. XVI, No. 4, March 5, 1972, p. 200.

8. T.K. Chakravarty, "Development of Small and Marginal Farmers: A Review of Politics and Programmes", Rural Development in India, some facts, National Institute of Rural Development, (Hyderabad, 1979), pp. 280-84.

9. Ibid.

10. Rural Development Directorate of Advertising and Visual Publicity, Ministry of Information and Broadcasting, Government of India, New Delhi, 1974, pp. 1-2.

11. Annual Report 1992-93, Government of India, Minsitry of Rural Development, Department of Rural Development (New Delhi, 1993), pp. 1-2.

12. Ibid.

13. *Gramin Vikas Newsletters.* A monthly journal of Ministry of Rural

Areas & Employment, Vol. 13, No. 2, February, 1997, (New Delhi), p. 8.

14. *Gramin Vikas Newsletter*, Vol. 1. No. 11, November 1985, op. cit., p. 4.

15. Ibid.

16. Ibid.

17. Ibid., p. 5.

18. Employment generation in 11 states were as such: Assam 41%, Gujarat 61%, Karnataka 56%, Kerala 60%, Madhya Pradesh 48%, Nagaland 94%, Meghalaya 74%, Orissa 43%, Tamil Nadu 42%, and almost all Union Territories also achieved the targets.

19. *Gramin Vikas News Letter*, Vol. 1, No. 2, November, 1985, op. cit., p. 6.

20. Ibid., p. 6.

21. Ibid.

22. Ibid., p. 7.

23. Ibid.

24. Ibid., p. 7.

25. V.M. Dandekar, and Nilkanth Rath, Poverty in India, (Bombay, 1971), p. 28.

26. Planning Commission, Government of India, Sixth Five Year Plan 1980-85, Annexure-1 and 12, p. 16.

6

Jawahar Rojgar Yojana: Its Objectives and Implementation

Since the Government of India under the leadership of Mrs. Indira Gandhi and also Rajiv Gandhi was very much committed to improve the vulnerable economic and social conditions of the rural people who were, in fact, socially suppressed and economically exploited, the government thought of some special economic schemes and programmes to provide special economic relief to these people. The government had already launched several schemes under the Integrated Rural Development Programme (IRDP). Before this there was Community Development Programmes which had failed to provide economic relief to the poor and down-trodden sections of the society. However, it has served as a base throughout the country to attract the people and involve them in development administration. The Panchayati Raj System was, in fact, the expansion and modification of the Community Development Programme. The IRDP incorporated in itself several plans and programmes for rural development. Special attention was paid to help the landless and unemployed rural families. The Village Panchayats and the Block Development Offices were organised with more power to assist Zila Parishad in implementing the Rural Development Programme. The aims and objectives of the Rural Development Agencies under the IRDP have already been discussed. However, it may be said that its main objectives were the same what the Community Development Programmes contained. The only difference was that the scope of the latter was limited to some recognised Blocks while the scope of the IRDP covered widely including all sects of the poor people living in the rural areas. With a view to expanding the scope of Rural Development and providing more economic relief and employment opportunity to the poor rural mass the government further launched a new Yojana, namely, Jawahar Rojgar Yojana.

According to the government official report the quantitative target had been fully achieved under the programmes adopted by IRDP, but observation revealed that there were namely shortcomings while giving practical shape to these programmes. These shortcomings included non-payment of minimum wages, delay in the payment of wages, low preference to women in employment, lack of maintenance plan and inventory of assets created and inadequate planning, lack of proper supervision and monitoring arrangements.[1] These short comings compelled the government to think about other ways or measures to help the rural poor.

Like the Sixth Five Year Plan the Seventh Five Year Plan also aimed at reducing the number of unemployed Persons in the rural areas. It emphasised food, work and productivity and decided to provide employment to everyone in the rural areas through the rural employment schemes under the National Rural Employment Programme and the Rural Landless Guarantee Employment Programme.[2] Now need was felt to introduce another programme which would provide employment to every one because the performance of the aforesaid programmes was defective and not so satisfactory. The Finance Minister of India in his Budget speech for the year 1989-90 announced a new scheme for intensive employment in backward districts with acute poverty and unemployment. Finance Minister further announced that to achieve the purpose and provide employment to everyone the government would make provision of Rs. 500/- crore. He also said that to spend the money allotted for, a new scheme, namely the Jawahar Rojgar Yojana (JRY) would be launched very soon.

The Jawahar Rojgar Yojana, was launched at the initiative of Rajiv Gandhi, the then Prime Minister of India. Like her mother, Mrs. Gandhi, he was also committed to the cause of poor. After her death he showed the concern for development of the backward and deprived sections of the people. He launched the programme with the intention to remove poverty from the country by providing employment to the unemployed rural people.

Under the JRY the expenditure was to be shared between the Centre and the States on 80:20 basis. Secondly, there is provision to release the Central share directly to the districts. Further, not less than 80 per cent of the allocation under the programme received by the district both as central assistance and the state contribution, are required to be given to the Village Panchayats. In other words, the assistance provided by the centre and the state should be spent through the Village Panchayats. This provision was made keeping in view that the villagers should get the benefits of the programme directly.

The government had been feeling that the villagers must be given opportunity to take direct participation in the development of the villages. They must be included the formulation of plans. In other words, the plans which were intended to develop the village economy and change the structure of the villages, should be prepared by the villagers with the assistance given by the government officials. Hence the JRY made provision for people's participation in the plan.

In 1989-90, the Finance Minister delivering the budget speech had announced that the National Rural Employment Programme and the Rural Landless Employment Guarantee Programme would be merged into the newly proposed scheme, the Jawahar Rojgar Yojana. Hence the Jawahar Rojgar Yojana comprised the schemes running under the NREP and RLEGP it was estimated that the new programme "will provide fuller employment opportunities to atleast one member of each family living below the poverty line who seek unskilled employment. It is also hoped that distribution of sources to village panchayats will result in increasing the coverage to all the rural areas and also ensure the fuller participation of the people in its implementation."[3]

Thus it is evident that the Jawahar Rojgar Yojana was launched with the intention to expand wide scope of employment on the one hand, and to provide for participation of the people in development programmes on the other. The JRY was more interested in providing employment to those poor masses who totally depend upon physical labour for their livelihood. There are several fields of work in the rural areas which require immediate improvement. The JRY stands for these works. Following are the list of works which can be taken up under the schemes of the JRY.

(i) Social forestry works on government and community lands belonging to panchayats etc., road side plantation along with canal banks or on wastelands, on side of railway lines etc., involving planning of fuels, fodder and fruits trees, distribution/sale of sampling for plantation on private lands, provided the sale proceeds are credited to respective Director of Rural Development Agencies and the same are ploughed back to JRY works.

(ii) Soil and water conservation works, water harvesting structures.

(iii) Minor irrigation works such as construction of community irrigation wells, construction of intermediary and main drains and fields, channels etc. and their improvements, depending etc.

(iv) Flood protection, drainage and water-lodging works.

(v) Construction/rennovation of village tanks for providing water for human use or cattle or for irrigation or pisciculture.

(vi) Irrigation wealth and field channels on individual holdings of members of SC/ST and allottees of ceiling surplus land, Bhoodan land and Government land.

(vii) Construction of institutional sanitary latriens in rural areas and institutional rural sanitation work like drains/ soakage pits near hand pumps/stand posts on community/institution basis.

(viii) Construction of houses for individual members of SC/ST and freed bounded labourers.

(ix) Construction of rural roads subject to prescribed standard and specification and in accordance with the MNP criteria.

(x) Land Development and reclamation of water land or degraded land with social emphasis in ecological improvement in hill and desert areas.

(xi) Augumenting existing ground water resources through micro level ecological planning involving aforestation, soil and moisture conservation and water management.

(xii) Construction of Rural Bank Buildings, Godowns for Storage or Inputs, community workshed for Target Group beneficiaries Community Centre, Panchayat Ghars, DWCRA Centres, Market Yards in Areas with concentration of Population of Weaker Section etc., and works which help the raising the resources for local panchayats through rents, market fees etc., so as to add to the overall resource availability for maintenance at the local level, may however be taken-up in preference to others.

(xiii) Works of a purely social and community nature such as dispensaries, panchayat ghars, community centres, creches, anganbaris, balwaris etc.

(xiv) The primary school buildings will be constructed on those revenue villages which have sanctioned schools without buildings of their own.[4]

Thus it is very much obvious that the working scope of the JRY is very large. It touches all the aspects of the rural construction. There is no scope of the Village Development or Development of the Rural Areas which have been left by the JRY. It covers ecological, educational, medical, sanitary and welfare aspects of the rural side. If these works are done properly, it will provide not only the jobs and employmetn to millions of the rural people who are yet unemployed but also change the economic face of the rural society. The condition of the rural India has been suffering from long. The face of rural area is still ugly. There are a number of villages which have no approach road or connected to the main road with the result that the villagers have to face a lot of problems specially during rainy season. Due to lacks of proper drainage system the people suffer from various kinds of diseases and their life is miserable. JRY takes into account all these problems of the rural areas. The main benefits of the JRY are mentioned below:

(i) The people in rural areas obtain the opportunity to avail supplementary employment.

(ii) It leads to alround development of villages.

(iii) It also improves the overall quality of life in the villages.[5]

One of the special features of the JRY is that both the men and women get enough scope and opportunity of employment. Rather thirty per cent jobs have been reserved for women only. This, in fact, increase the living standard of the family and makes the life of the family somewhat more prosperous and happy. The works which are done for the community as a whole are, in fact, beneficial to every one. These works not only change the shape and beauty of the villages but also provide several facilities and conveniences to the villagers which are very much essential and significant for their happy life. The provisions for angnwari and balwari provide opportunity to the adult and illiterate for manfolk to learn basic things of life. The children who are unable to get education in the schools are benefited by balwaris. The lands which are useless in the rural areas or the land which are wastelands are utilised by the scheme where various kinds of plants are planted which beautifies the rural areas on one hand and helps to maintain ecological balance on the other.

Under the well planned scheme of JRY both the men and women belonging to backward and poor sections of the society were given ample opportunity to obtain employment living in their own home. Rather 30 per cent jobs have been reserved for the ladies keeping in view their negligible condition. Moreover, the works which have been included in the JRY began to change the face of the villages. These changes provided them more comfort removing inconveniences which they have been facing before. The JRY created much hope among the villagers and they became more and more option taking part in such activities.

The JRY, in fact, is a recent drive of the central government aiming at placing in the hands of the villages Panchayats around the country adequate financial fund to run their own rural employment schemes in the interest of the vast masses of the rural poor who constitute the bulk of the Rural India. Before the introduction of the JRY only 55 per cent of the villages had been benefitted from the Rural Employment Programme such as the NREP and RLEGP. So the JRY aimed at reaching every Panchayat and involving every member of the families which wanted employment or manual work as part time jobs. It provided addition fund for employment generation. The Central Government, in the beginning, provided Rs. 2100 crore to meet the needs. There is provision to give every Panchayat at least Rs. one lakh in a year to be spent on the development of the villages on the area of the works marked already. It can be noted that village Panchayats are being regarded as the most important unit for Rural Development. So it is to be given some more autonomies. The JRY functions under the Village Panchayats. The Village Panchayats are the main centre round which all the activities of the JRY circulate. Though the Panchayats have to prepare the plans for development under the direction of the Zila Parishad, they have autonomies to choose and pick their preferences of works in the meeting of the Gram Sabha where every adult members of the Panchayat has the right to participate and express his opinion or to suggest priority of works keeping in view general welfare and well being of villagers. Thus planning are adopted from the grass-root level where preference is given to the opinions of the villagers who are to harvest the benefits of development works. The officials of the Development Blocks help the villagers to take decision according to the fund provided.

There is plan to entrust the village panchayats with the task of formulating schemes of employment generation.

The JRY proposed to benefit those members of the rural areas or households who presently get employment for less than six months in a year due to non-availability of works in the villages. One member of such each family is provided employment for 50 to 100 days in a year. Moreover, "the Yojana is intended to reach out to every corner of the country and to the 440 lakhs families in rural India living below the poverty line."[16]

No doubt, the JRY is a right drive in right time. It is a device to provide economic relief to the poor family and change the ugly face of the villages into beautiful face. It is also true that it has awakened a number of villagers whose economic conditions are vulnerable and whose living standard is lamantable. But it all depends upon the implementation of programmes and sincerity and honesty of the people who are directly associated with implementation of the works. The main objectives of the JRY are to provide maximum economic relief to the people of the rural areas and also to bring about major change in the physical structure of the villages and their surroundings. This Yojana has been launched keeping in view the poor results of the schemes adopted under the IRDP, NREP and RLEGP. The aim of the JRY is high and its scope is wider. But the results of the JRY what have been observed so far are not hopeful. These results envisage that the expectations which people have from the Yojana have not yet been fulfilled. The scheme has been running for more than a decade, but the results achieved through its schemes are not encourageable. It produces sad and dark picture has it happened in other schemes. It is true that the JRY has remained successful in many villages. It is also true that it has remained successful in changing the shape of the village and providing some relief to the villagers. Several villages have been found moving towards prosperity. They have been linked with main roads through construction of approach roads. So far plantation of trees in the Rural Areas or alongside the main roads, railway lines etc. are concerned, some notable progress has been noted. The Yojana has provided some employment to the poor villagers and their economic condition has improved in comparison to their past economic life.[7] The part time jobs provided under the JRY have enabled them to maintain at least minimum standard of life. When the JRY was launched, it had created new hope and aspiration among the poor and field workers. Today their hopes and aspirations have been dampened due to mismanagement of the whole affairs.[8]

A general survey of working of the JRY specially in Bihar and Uttar Pradesh, revel as the fact that the funds allotted by the government to run the schemes is not sufficient keeping in view the number of the poor families and the number of the family members. Secondly, most of the Village Panchayats in India, specially in the State like Bihar, Uttar Pradesh, Orissa, Madhya Pradesh and Rajasthan are either defunct or inactive with the result that the JRY has not received proper attention. The villagers in the absence of village Panchayats do not get opportunity to participate in the meetings do not get opportunity to participate in the meetings and decide the priority of works. It is the government officials sitting in the Blocks and in the office of the Zila Parishad who take the decisions and sanction the amounts. The villagers are mere witnesses. It has been observed in Bihar that the Village Panchayats have not been constituted for more than a decade. There is no Mukhiya or Pradhan. Hence the programmes of the JRY have not got proper direction according to the need priority of the people.

Thirdly, the officers and workers related to the JRY for implementation of its various schemes and programmes are not committed to the objective of the JRY. They perform their duties in this regard half-heartedly. Moreover, the wide corruption prevailed among the government officials and workers from top to bottom of the administrative machinery has further badly affected the success of the JRY. These officers and workers do not hesitate to take undue benefits of the schemes by throwing dust into the eyes of the general mass. They have fixed their share every where in the name of commission at the rate of prescribed percentage. Their such dishonest and irresponsible behaviours have, in fact, badly damaged the sanctity of the JRY on the one hand, and deeply affected its targets. Fourthly, the mass illiteracy prevailed among the poor people of the rural areas has always been a hard barrier between the them and the government. These illiterate persons take considerable amount of time to grasp the significance of economic development programme and understand the objectives of the schemes. Moreover, the officers and workers concerned take undue benefits of their illiteracy and laziness. In fact, most of the backward and suppressed villagers have not yet fully understood the significance and objectives of such economic development schemes. The lack of the knowledge of procedure how to get benefits and whom to contact with the result that they have to depend upon some agents who directly or indirectly exploit them by taking their shares.

Fifthly, the rural workers, in fact, need full time employment, no part time. They cannot wait to get benefits of the part time employment because they are in constant search for jobs which they get at different places.

Thus it is clear that the JRY like other rural development schemes and projects have not yet achieved commendable results to eradicate poverty from India or at least to reduce poverty. In fact, the JRY was a device adopted by the government to mobilise the rural lot by providing economic relief to the poor.

Technically the JRY is good, its objects are appreciable, but it lacks the real will power of the government. Until the government is deeply committed to eradicate poverty from the country, the desired result cannot be achieved. Unemployment in India is increasing day by day. According to an estimate of the Planning Commission of India, in March, 1980 itself, 34.75 million people were unemployed on the basis of usual status, 35.18 million on the weekly status and 59.68 million on the basis of daily status.[9] Today in the country nearly 750 million people are need of jobs to meet their requirements of daily life. The unemployment in India is increasing at the rate of more than one lakh per month.

Poverty eradication and employment generation have always been the two key objectives of India's development strategy since independence. Growth of the economy and specific target-oriented poverty alleviation programmes have been tried as major tools. There has always been a difference among Indian economists and planner, however, on whether `growth per se' can solve the poverty problems or whether a specific redistribution of policy is also needed to meet this objective. The realised growth of economy was very low right through until the mid-1970s, and no opportunity therefore arise to test the so-called 'percolation theory of growth' hypotheses. The economy did not shift from the low Hindu rate of growth of around 3.5 per cent to above 5.5 per cent per annum until the 1980s. This was also the period when poverty decreased and the government launched a large number of target-oriented poverty alleviation programmes. Poverty reduction during this period may therefore be ascribed both to growth and redistributive measures.

Poverty is multi-dimensional concept, and 'poor' is defined in many ways in contemporary literature. No specific definition or measurement is fullproof. The most commonly used measurement in India is from the 'consumption angle', that is, whether the money for consumption available to a house-hold or individual enables the purchase of food that will satisfy a minimum'calorie-value' agreed on the basis of FAO norms in the total basket of purchase. Calorie norms are stipulated by rural and urban per capita, determined by the colorie requirement of an individual given his/her gender, age and occupation, to lead an active life.[10]

An analysis of the results of the various poverty alleviation programmes from 1980s onwards shows that the percentage of secondary and tertiary employment in the rural sector has declined. Whenever there is a lack of activity, rural labour mostly moves to agriculture. This in some sense corroborates our earlier findings that unemployment must have increased in agriculture.

The Government of India has committed itself to the concept of reform with a human face and has promises to device several safety net measures. Apart from the PDS, there is the national renewal fund (NRF). This a recent addition to India's social safety net, having received considerable attention in the context of contemporary debates on policy reform on employment and labour laws. In creating the NRF, the Union Finance Minister declared that government will fully protect the interest of labour inhance their welfare and equip them in all aspects to deal with the inevitability of technological change. The NRF was official established in February 1992. It currently functions as a government budgetary account, administered by the department of Industrial Development in the Ministry of Industry. The NRF operates under a set of guidelines to be approved by the cabit, which stipulates the objectives, use of funds, staffing and other aspects. Two specific human resource objectives are directly addressed through the NRF. The first, known as the National renewal grant fund (NRGF) is used, wherever necessary, to compensate workers who become dislocated in the process of adjusting organisational staffing patterns, or enclosing non-viable units in the public and private sectors. The second, the employment generation fund (EGF), will be used to facilitate the re-employment and re-training of affected workers and to fund specific initiative of employment generation in areas affected workers and to fund specific initiatives of employment generation in areas affected by industrial restructuring and technological upgrading.

Thus the programmes for poverty alleviation are still on run. The government is alert and effective measures are being searched out and adopted to improve the implementation of programmes. It is expected that the struggle of the government against mass poverty which has covered the country, will continue and desired results would be achieved.

References

1. Hugh Tinker, "The Village in the Framework of Development", in Ralph Braibanti and Joseph J., (eds), Administration and Economic Development in India, (London, 1963), pp. 45-48.

2. Planning Commission of India, Seventh Five Year Plan, Government of India, New Delhi, p. 135.

3. Manual of Jawahar Rojgar Yojana, issued by the Department of Rural Development, Ministry of Agriculture, Government of India (New Delhi), August, 1989, pp. 12-13.

4. Jawahar Rojgar Yojana, Manual, Department of Rural Development, Ministry of Agriculture, op. cit., pp. 26-27.

5. Jawahar Rojgar Yojana, Ministry of Agriculture, Rural Development Department, Published by State Resource Centre, Jamia Milia Islamia, New Delhi, 1989, p. 2.

6. *Gramin Vikas Newsletters,* Vol. 5, No. 8-9, op. cit., p. 19.

7. Based on personal survey of the area in the villages where JRY is run specially in Bihar.

8. Based on personal interviews with the beneficiaries of the Scheme in rural areas.

9. The Government of India, Planning Commission, Sixth Five Year Plan, 1980-85, (New Delhi, 1981), p. 204.

10. C.H. Hanumantha Rao and Hans Linnemann (Eds), Economic Reforms and Poverty Alleviation in India, (New Delhi, 1996), pp. 127-28.

7

Recent Special Central Schemes for Development of Rural Poor

Special attention for rural development by launching new projects and schemes under various agencies was paid first by the Congress Government under the leadership of Mrs. Indira Gandhi during National Emergency in 1975. No doubt, the Indian National Congress had been talking a lot for establishment of egalitarian society even before independence of India. The Congress in its various Annual Conferences passed several resolutions putting special emphasis on 'Socialistic Pattern of Society'.[1] Under the leadership of Pt. Jawaharlal Nehru the Indian National Congress had laid down the foundation of Socialistic Pattern of Society as early as in 1955 at Avadi Session of the Congress. In the wake of this policy of the Congress Government during the regime of Mrs. Indira Gandhi want on giving effect to the policy of the socialistic pattern of society despite a number of hurdles caused by the conservative forces and vested interests. No doubt, the Government took up various steps first to abolish the practices of the capitalistic pattern of society whereby some Acts and ordinances were passed to abolish the practice of Landlordism and Privy Purse.[2] Mrs. Gandhi also nationalised fourteen major Commercial Banks with a view to channelising the economic funds towards rural development despite though opposition from the conservative forces and vested elements.[3]

Under this very spirit the Congress Government went on adopting various policies and launching schemes to eradicate poverty from India by helping the down-trodden and suppressed sections of the society which have already been discussed in the preceeding chapters. The Government spent huge amount of money over these schemes and projects. During the regime of Ex-Prime Minister Narasimha Rao, some more agencies, though volunteer, appeared to work for development of the poor. The Government of Narasimha Rao, too launched some special programmes to help the deprived sections of the society. Before discussing about such special agencies and new trends of the Government for Rural Development it would be more convenience if a short discussion is made about emergence of new volunteer agencies and their works.

Rural development in India has been taken as a movement aiming at eradicating poverty from the rural scene. So there are not only the government machinery and agencies to work for the rural development but also some voluntary organisations which ae playing vital role in helping the rural people. These voluntary organisations working in the rural fields are assisted by the People's Action for Development India (PADI) which was organised by the Government nearly three decades back. It is a nodal organisation for voluntary agencies which is actively engages in promoting voluntary efforts. PADI aims at providing financial assistance to voluntary organisations to implement rural development projects, taking the initiative in promoting the voluntary agencies and building up local leadership and organising training for voluntary organisations rural workers and beneficiaries. It was set-up mainly for canalising funds from foreign sources. Till 1984 it was not depending upon the government for funds. It was actively associated with the implementation of the programme of Development of Women and Children in Rural Areas (DWCRA) and Promotion of Voluntary Schemes and Social Action Programme.

The DWCRA, as a sub-scheme of IRDP, was launched by the Department of Rural Development in the middle of the Sixth Plan. No doubt, the DWCRA came into being in 1982-84, but it came in actual practice only from 1983-84. One year was devoted to "identification of participants, economic projects, selection of staff, training of participants and functionaries and other allied works."[4] Soon after its implementation, the programme got wide appreciation and response from the public. The total number of groups formed during the Sixth Plan were 3,308 with membership of 52,170. The Central and UNICEF share released for DRDA was Rs. 335.85 lakhs. The State Governments also contributed to the scheme. In the first year of the Seventh Plan, a target of 4,860 groups was fixed for 50 selected districts.[5] Thus the PADI is getting now central assistance for implementing DWCRA in rural areas. The Central Government have decided to help the voluntary organisations through the PADI because the roles played by them have been fully recognised by the government. PADI organised a conference of leading voluntary organisations on the 5th and 6th June 1985 to disseminate the programme, generate project proposals and decide modalities of implementing the scheme of assistance to the voluntary agencies. It has been organising regional conferences of voluntary agencies for finding out means and ways to develop rural areas. Thus with the help of the PADI the voluntary organisations are active in rural development. But there are some voluntary agencies which main aim is to get fund from the government and devour it up in the name of rural development.

Thus it is very much obvious that Integrated Rural Development Programme which came into being from early eighties with massive programmes to remove poverty from the Rural India has become very much popular all over the country. This programme has covered both the districts plains and the hills. In the hills districts where mostly tribal people live more attention has been given. The movement of rural development through IRDP has created new hope and aspirations among the people specially belonging to the poor sections.

The latest approach to the development in India is Integrated rural development. It is now recognised that development does not merely imply an increase in GNP or per capita income. The increased income should be so distributed as to reduce the inequalities in income and wealth. It is the right approach specially in a country like India where the maximum number of people are very poor and where the government is committed to the principle of socialistic pattern of society. Moreover, development does not mean an increase in wealth and property. Development means change in the living style, thinking aspect, behaviour, etc. Development is expected to include areas of health, education, culture and values of life. Again, mere provision of opportunities for development is not enough. Creation of facilities necessary for actual utilization of these opportunities is also imperative. It is the integrated development approach which is committed to all these factors. A.K. Pandey has rightly pointed out that "integrated development really means the development of areas and the people through optimum development utilization of local resources and by bringing about necessary institutional, structural and attitudinal changes and by delivering a package of services to include all fields of activity."[6] The IRDP in India pays special attention to the rural poor and the rural weak. The target group for the IRDP in India is more inclined towards small and marginal farmers, share croppers, landless labourers and rural artisans. The entire machinery is busy with implementing various programmes and projects of the IRDP. There are various problems on the way of implementation. Success relies upon the awareness, and activities of the general masses, sincerity and honesty of the government officials connected with the programmes and the public leaders who are responsible for development of the country as a whole.

The Government of Mrs. Indira Gandhi, in 1975, had launched a programme, namely, 20-Point Economic Programme. It was this programme which was called as 'A New Economic Deal'. After her death, her son, Rajeev Gandhi, added some more points to give a decisive push to the economic policy of the country.[7] But due to political upheavals and her defeat in the parliamentary Election of 1977, these programmes had not been given effect. The centrally Sponsored Schemes launched by the Government of India to eradicate poverty and change the economic rural face of India, the 20-Point Economic Programme served as a theoretical source. It was this programme which put emphasis on strengthening and expanding "Coverage of Integrated Rural Development and National Rural Employment Programmes." It also put emphasis on the review and effectively reinforce minimum wages for agricultural labour, to accelerate programme for development of Scheduled Castes and Scheduled Tribes. The programme further emphasized on accelerating programmes of welfare for women and children and nutrition programmes for pregnant women, nursing mothers and children specially in tribal hills backward areas. Special attention was paid to spread universal elementary education for the age-group of 6-14 with special emphasis on girls and simultaneously involve students and voluntary agencies in programmes for the removal of adult illiteracy from the country. Need was realised to expand public distribution system through more fair-price shops, including mobile shops in far flung areas and shops to cater to industrial workers, student hostels, and make available to student text-books and exercise books on a priority basis and to promote a strong consumer protection movement.

Thus it is evident that the attention of the Government was paid to exploit all possible economic resources and work for the poorest of the poor all over the country. No doubt, the progrmmes and schemes under the Integrated Rural Development Programme (IRDP) all the aforesaid programmes were included. The Jawahar Rojgar Yojana, specially put much emphasis on providing employment to those agricultural labourers who do not get opportunity to have employment all round the year. But it is notable that the schemes launched by the central government in this regard were not sufficient. Hence there was more scope to work for eradicating poverty and assisting the poorest of the poor in India.

During the regime of the Prime Ministership of P.V. Narasimha Rao, the Congress governed adopted some new centrally sponsored schemes in favour of the poor people living in the villages. One such schemes is the Indira Awas Yojana. In fact, one of the most crucial problems of the rural and urban poor is the living accommodation the poor people. Almost in villages the down-trodden and suppressed sections of people have no house of their own for living. Some of those who have their houses have no sufficient rooms and other facilities like drinking water, electricity, proper drainge etc. It has been observed that millions of people are either without houses or their small houses are nothing but huts in very poor condition. The walls of these houses are mud-made and their roofs are thatched. During rainy season such huts are not fit for human habitation. Most of such thatched *kacha* buildings are eiher fall down on the ground or full of water leakage. Moreover, these houses are without proper door or windows. There is no safety at all. The owners of such houses are too poor to repair their houses or rebuild them. As a result, they have to suffer all round the year.

In absence of good buildings the poor inhabitants suffer from various kinds of diseases such as Cholera, Dysentry, dyspepsia, T.B. etc. Due to lack of proper sanitation and nutrition they frequently fall victim to such diseases and they have to loose their lives sometimes. Some of the rural workers have to serve under perpetual bondage of their masses because of the land and houses provided to them by their masses. Keeping in view all these problems and difficulties of the depressed poor the Government of India started the Indira Awas Yojana.

Under the Indira Awas Yojana there is provision to construct small *pacca* buildings with proper drainage and other facilities on the cost of the Government for those who are below the line of poverty. The selection of the occupants of the Indira Awas is made by the village panchayat and the Block areas with the help of the Zila Parishad.

This scheme in fact, provide and is still providing too much relief to the people of the poor sections. The Government of India has spent millions of Rupees over these schemes. This has covered the whole of the country. Lakhs of Buildings have been constructed and allotted to the poor families who were living in conjusted space. But keeping in view the number of the poor families, the houses constructed under the Indira Awas Yojana are not enough. Millions of people are still in need of such help. Secondly, the drawback of the buildings constructed under the Yojana is that they very small in size and have a few rooms which are not sufficient for a big family. Thirdly, the money is not spent honestly on the construction of the buildings with the result that the buildings are not durable. Fourthly, while selecting the names of the occupants of the buildings, there is too much mal-adjustment and favourtism. It has been observed that a number of persons who are above the poverty line and have access to the authorities concerned, have succeeder in getting undue benefit from the Indira Awas Yojana.[8] Fifthly, only those persons are selected for buildings who have their own land for construction of the buildings under the Indira Awas Yojana. Many persons belonging to the labourer class have no land of their own, with the result that they are deprived of such facilities. Therefore the Yojana needs amendments in it. The poor people should be provided the land free of cost for construction of buildings under such scheme.

The another scheme launched under the leadership of P.V. Narashmiha Rao to help the children of the poor sections in getting Primary Education was to provide one meal every day to the school going children specially in the rural areas. The most of the children of the manual workers are deprived of Primary Education because of two factors. Firstly, their parents are too poor to offered even a small expenditure on the primary study of their children. Secondly, these children are employed at various manual jobs to help their parents. Hence, they do not get time to attend schools. Keeping in view these two factors the government of Narasimha Rao planned to attract the poor children towards primary educations. Instructions have been passed to the concerned school managements to distribute food among them free of cost. Provision has also been made to give them school dress and text-books either on subsidised rate or without cost.

An observation of this running scheme brings about very sad results. The scheme has been launched in haphazard manner, without giving due consideration to the part of its implementation.

As a result, the beneficiaries are yet deprived of real benefit of the scheme. The School Management are not implementing the scheme honestly. Their intention is to pocket the money net of the fund provided for the scheme. The number of the students admitted in schools are false. They produce false lists comprising a number of false names of students just to obtain maximum fund. Secondly, despite the facilities provided to them the children of the poor family are still reluctant to attend the schools. It is all because either they do not get enough spared time to attend the school or the school does not run properly. It has been observed that the most of the schools established in rural areas are without buildings. Those who have buildings are without furniture and proper number of teachers. The teachers available in the school are not committed to their duties. They are neither regular nor punctual. Due to all these factors children have no interest in the schools maintained by the government. The supervising and controlling authorities hardly take interest to supervise the schools of the rural areas and control the teachers therein.[9]

Besides these schemes the Government of India as well as the State Governments have launched some more new schemes to help the poor women, the unmarried girls and widows. Dowry has remained a great hurdle and social evil in the Indian society. That is why the girls have remained neglected subject in each family. Hence to help girls and women the postal insurance scheme and Recurring Deposit Scheme in the post-office with special relief from the Government for them was launched by the government. Under such scheme the women were encouraged to open their saving accounts in the nearest post offices with small savings. The amount put in the post office in the women, girls and widows are doubled within every limited period of time, with the help of the Government. It was expected that such money would help them when they needs and every women would have their own savings which would improve their status in the society.

The scheme is very good, no doubt, but it could not produce the desired result due to various factors. Firstly, this scheme also was launched haphazardly by the government of Narsimha Rao.

The rural intention of the government behind the scheme was not to help the women and upgrade their status, but to achieve popularity of the Government. Secondly, the most of the rural women not failed to understand the significance of such scheme. Thirdly, they are not in position to deposit even a minimum amount in saving account in Post Offices. Those who opened saving accounts too, could not run it to the stage of maturity. As a result, this scheme has almost failed all over the country.

With the help of Government a number of Anganwaris have been opened in the Rural areas to educate the rural women. Most of the rural women are illiterate. It was thought that these women would not be made through this scheme only literate but also aware of civilised life. The scheme is good in itself, no doubt, but like other schemes this also has brought about disappointing result. In fact this has became mere a device to pocket the Government fund by the vested interests. A number of Anganwaris and some other institutions in the rural areas are running on paper. There is a net of brokers and corrupt government servants related to these schemes who are managing successfully to have major portion of the fund allotted with the result that the rural women have not been helped as per the plan.

Thus it is very much obvious that despite a number of projects, programmes and schemes to remove poverty from the rural areas and to help the rural people, the government has failed in this regard. Mass prevailed corruption among the government servants and their traditional bureaucratics attitude as well as ignorance of the rural people are the major factors responsible for perpetuation of poverty in the rural areas. The Indian society is not yet free from parasitic elements who move round the machinery of the government and its several agencies in the guise of the best citizens of the country. V.M. Dandekar and Nilkanth Rath, while examining how the benefits of developments were shared between different sections of population, came to the conclusion that the process of development in the rural section "has benefited the upper middle and the richer sections much more than the middle, the lower middle and the poorer sections."[10] The 6th Plan Commission has also accepted that around 50% of the population of India lives below the poverty line facing a number of difficulties and inconvenience.[11] The rich have become richer and the poor have become poorer. The schemes like Co-operative Farmings, Joint Co-operative Farming, CDP, IRDP, JRY etc. have remained failure. The unemployment is increasing day-by-day. The amount for giving subsidies to the poor in general and to the Harijans and Adivasi's in particular are not reaching to them.

The measures adopted by the Government to remove poverty and reduce inequalities, no doubt, have provided some relief to the poor sections, but no marked change has been caused in day-to-day life of the millions of half-nacked and starving people in the rural areas. In the words of Chandrika Singh "It is all because widely prevalence of nepotism, favouritism and corruption make the deserving suffering masses to get the due benefit of these schemes. The administrative machinery of the government remained so loose, inactive and corrupt that it failed to control the practice of mass corruption."[12]

References

1. Pattabhi Sitaramaya, *The History of the Indian National Congress 1885-1935*, Vol. I, p. 343.

   Also see, Indian National Congress Resolution on Fundamental Rights and Economic Programme, The Karachi Session, 1931.

2. Chandrika Singh, Socialism in India: Rise, Growth and Perspective (New Delhi, 1986), pp. 138-42.

3. *Kesvanand Bharti Vs. State of Kerala*, 1973 Sc. 1461, Para 759, 850, 1474, 1582, and 1595.

4. *Gramin Vikas Newsletter*, Vol. I, No. 11, November, 1985, op. cit., p. 8.

5. *Ibid.*, p. 8.

6. A.K. Pandey, *Local Level Planning and Rural Development*, op. cit., p. 116.

7. For detail study of 20 Point Economic Programme, See Chandrika Singh, Socialism in India, op. cit., pp. 191-93.

8. Based on Personal Survey of the Building Construction under IAY. (Indira Awas Yojana).

9. Based on Personal Survey of some schools of the Rural Areas and Personal Interviews with the Rural Parents and Guardians of the school going children.

10. V.M. Dandekar & Nilkanth Rath, Poverty in India (Bombay, 1971), page 28.

11. Government of India, Planning Commission 6th Five Year Plan, 1980-1985, Annexure 1, 12, p. 16.

12. Chandrika Singh, *Socialism in India: Rise Growth and Prospect*, op. cit., p. 207.

8

Political and Administrative Changes

Development and administration are closely related. Development and mass common welfare have remained basic objectives of the welfare government. The plannings, schemes, projects etc. of a government to change the socio-economic face of a society or to constitute and egalitarian society can not be implemented until administrative branch of the government is efficient enough. No developmental scheme can be implemented fully and efficiently without strong, smart, honest and active administrators. If administrators are corrupt and inactive or non-interested in the welfare scheme, nothing remarcably can be achieved. Moreover, corruption in administration is like a paralysis. Much depends upon the will and interest of the administrators who are made responsible for implementing development schemes people's participation in administration is also a valid point. Today when government is committed to change the socio-economic face of the people and rural areas, it has become much more important to allow the people to participate in development administration.

Development administration is a global term today and it has become an integral part of the government which is democratically formed and inclined to socialistic principles. So far the case of Indian Government is concerned, the Indian constitution provides socialistic pattern of society. Part fourth of the constitution, namely, Directive Principles of State Policy, Stands for giving effect to a society based on the principles of democratic socialism.

Keeping in views the aims and objectives of the constitution, various changes have been brought in India's administrative frame work. After independence, the government had constituted the Department of Agriculture to make derived changes in the agrarian field. As the years rolled down and the government adopted various plans and projects to remove poverty from the rural areas and improve the living standard of the poor masses, the need was felt to bring about effective charges in administrative pattern of the country. The government of India created new Department of Rural Development and Constituted a number of Development blocks supported with technically efficient administrative staff with a view to giving effect to the policies of development in rural areas. The Community Development Project became main administrative centre of India. Thereafter, following the recommendations of Ashok Mehta Committee the government decentralised the power and empowered the village panchayats to share in a development administration. This chapter discuss all these factors in detail and examines how far development administration has been affected by mass prevailed corruption.

The term development administration, a cosmopolitan political concept, is basically associated with the democratic and socialistic principles. It got considerable amount of strength with the rise of 'Welfare State' in the later part of the nineteenth century. Expansion of socialism based on the Marxist principles made the development administration indispensable for each State. Since welfare to the general mass is the basic motive of each State today, development administration of priority all over the world. The States devoted to the democratic and socialistic principles directly or indirectly introduced development administration with a view to doing more welfare to the people with the result that numerous people have been involved to development administration. It has opened broader scope for people's participation in administration. On the other hand, investment or large amount of funds to the development administration to give practical shape to various development schemes and projects has not only expanded the infra-structure of administrative machinery but has also opened new scope of corruption. In India, it were the British rulers who had laid down the foundation of development administration, no doubt, but their main objective behind it was to strength on the district administration for collection of revenue. However, the foundation given by them in this regard became guiding factor for the Indian rulers after independence.

Development administration in India got prominence only after independence through the Five Year Plans which gradually opened new dimension of development administration framing various development projects, schemes and programmes all over the country to achieve the declared goal of the Indian constitution which talks out to secure justice to all the citizens without any discrimination.[2] The objectives of the present chapter are to discuss and analyse the increasing scope of development administration in India, people's participation in it and attitudes of the administrators who are directly or indirectly associated with development administration.

People's participation in India in development administration began with launching of the Community Development Project in 1952 which wanted to make "considerable increase in agricultural production and more specially, production of food grains and development of village and small scale industries."[3] On the advice of the Planning Commission the Government of India started to provide technical advice, supply needs for better cultivation and grant loans to the farmers through nation-wide Community Development Programme.[4] The basic objectives of the C.D.P. were:

1. Development with a minimum all-round progress;
2. Self-help programme; and
3. Development of the whole community with special emphasis on to give preference to the weaker and under privileged sections for self-development.[5]

With the establishment of the Ministry of Community Development in 1956, the C.D.P. got wider strength, Many Blocks under the Block Development Officers (B.D.Os) were set up in various parts of the country which linked a number of the rural people with administration. A new scheme to be called as 'National Extension Services' was also launched to guide and control the village development schemes in each Block. The B.D.O. was supported with various types of technical and non-technical staff. Thus the Community Development Programme and National Extension Services became pioneers in the field of rural development of India. However, the main thrust of these schemes and projects yet remained confined to achieve the established targets rather than to do welfare to the general mass.[6]

The success and popularity of the aforesaid schemes and projects which boosted the morale of both the Government and the people, encouraged the Government to appoint the Balvant Ray Mehta Committee to investigate into the working of these schemes and suggest some more viable ways and means to expand the scope for participation of more and more people in development administration. The Committee during investigation found that the Government officials working under such schemes and projects "followed a hierarchic bureaucratic trend with the result that even a Gram Sevak instead of moving through villages,.... began to expect villagers to come to their offices for their requirements."[7] In the words of B.B. Misra, "Those who were expected to act as pioneer in a new venture of national-building became more cogs in the traditional bureaucratic machine, losing all sense of drive and initiative."[8] The Mehta Committee recorded that the very objectives of the C.D.P. to establish close contact with the rural people and encourage them to participate in local development planning and its implementation had been lost.[9] The Committee with a view to putting check upon mounting bureaucratic and hierarchic tendencies in India and expanding more scope for people's participation in administration, recommended a new policy based on `democratic decentralisation' on the national scale. It recommended for establishment of three-tier Panchayati Raj system of administration for rural development. The Village Panchayat was recommended to serve as the lowest pattern of village administration while the Zila Parishad was proposed to act as the supervisory and guiding body sitting at the top at the district level with the District Magistrate as its Ex-official Chairman.[10] There was a proposal for formation a Block Samiti, too, to act as a middle body between the Village Panchayat and the Zila Parishad.

The Mehta Committee's view of 'decentralisation' meant "a process whereby the Government divests itself completely of certain duties and responsibilities" and to extent them "to some other authority." In other words, the Committee suggested the democratically instituted local bodies in the rural areas should be allowed to work independently without undue interference from the bureaucrats.[11] In the opinion of the Committee the officials sitting at the top should perform the job of 'guidance' to 'avoid making mistake' by the local bodies. That is why it recommended that the District Magistrate or Collector should preside over the deliberations of the Zila Parishad with one of its officers acting as its secretary.[12]

No doubt, the three-tier Panchayati Raj System was introduced in maximum states of India on the line suggested by the Mehta Committee. It opened wide scope for people's participation in local administration. But these local institutions lacked required financial support, and secondly, there were several sections of the people such as artisans, field workers, small farmers etc. who were yet deprived of the opportunity to obtain benefits of the democratically decentralized rural institutions. It was marked that the afluent class of the society became more active and succeeded in establishing their hold over Village Panchayats and Samitis. On the other hand, the people belonging to the lower sections of the society remained either inactive or unable to occupy the required place. Moreover, corruption increased and prevailed among both the government officials related to the Panchayati Raj System and the democratically elected people of the system. As a result, the required established objectives of the Panchayati Raj System could not be achieved.[13]

It is true that the decisive and effective way to check up the growth of bureaucratic elitism and totalitarianism is to enable maximum number of people to participate in administration at grass-root level. They should participate in decision-making process, in implementation or development of programmes and project and sharing the benefits of such programmes and projects. Now the Government of India by seventies of this century began to think about how to create environment for participation of maximum number of people in local fields specially in the rural one.[14] So as a device, since the seventies the emphasis "shifted from agriculture, and rural development was defined as a strategy designed to improve the economic and social life of a specific group of people living in rural areas."[15] Consequently, the new policy of the Government began to cover not only the farmers and agricultural labourers but those persons also who were still neglected and living below the line of poverty. There were different agencies working for multiplicity of programmes for rural masses. Now these different agencies were brought under single integrated programme which covered all aspects of the rural life all over the country. It was called `Integrated Rural Development Programme' IRDP). Thus the IRDP in the form of `single largest anti-thrust' emerged during the Sixth Five Year Plan (1978-83) opening wide scope for people's participation in development administration.

In fact, IRDP was a multi-dimensional programme which integrated development of the rural areas and the rural people "through optimum development and utilisation of the local resources—physical, biological and human and bringing necessary institutional, structural and attitudinal changes by delivering a package of services to encompass not only the economic field, but also the establishment of the required social infra-structure and services in the areas of health and nutrition etc."[16] It was a nation-wide movement, stimulated and guided by the Government of India which influenced people from all sections. It is evident from the statement of the Planning Commission which inter alia said the Government was committed for giving "a practical shape to the nation's collective will for using all the latent resources and energies of the nation for an effective attack on poverty, unemployment and inequalities."[17]

The IRDP came into being in 1980 which soon covered all the 5011 Blocks of the Nation, various rural development programmes were brought under a single agency known as the District Rural Development Agency (DRDA). Thousand of the Government officials got involved in giving practical shape to the objectives of the IRDP. While inaugurating the National Development Council conference on November 8, 1986 at New Delhi, the Prime Minister of India, said that "Our anti-poverty programmes constitute the core of the 20-Point Programme. These will be expanded and restricted to give maximum assistance to families below poverty line."[18] Regarding the people's participation in these programmes the Prime Minister said, "We must involve the people in implementing these programmes. A new life has to be breathed into decentralized institutions."[19]

The components of the IRDP, namely, the Industry Service and Business (ISB) and the Training of Rural Youth for Self-Employment (TRYSEM) were brought into forçe with a view to helping the rural youths in obtaining self-employment in various fields with the help of the Government. Provisions for giving youths training for driving, knitting and embroidery etc. were made on large scale all over the nation with stippends and subsidy money.[20] Again, to provide supplementary employment to the underdeveloped and undeveloped rural landless youths, two special schemes, namely, National Rural Employment Programme (NREP) and Rural Landless Employment Programme (RLEP) were launched in 1980 and in 1983 respectively. The Government of India sanctioned crores of rupees to give practical shape to all these programmes.[21] Thereafter, one more new scheme called as Jawahar Rojgar Yojana (JRY) was also introduced with the objectives to "provide fuller employment opportunities to at least one member of each family living below the poverty line who seek unskilled employment," and to "ensure the fuller participation of people in its implementation."[22]

Thus it is very much obvious that the Government of India adopted various methods and schemes which opened wide scope for people's participation in development administration. No doubt, people welcomed these schemes and programmes with great enthusism and took active part also to improve their economic condition. It is also true that these schemes and programmes benefited numerous persons and families providing self-employment of them. The schemes and programmes are still in practice. But it is discouraging to note that the target fixed by the Government to be achieved through these programmes could not be achieved. Poverty and unemployment are yet to be removed. There are millions of poor people who are yet deprived of the opportunity to get employment and serve their daily needs. One may raise a question here as to why did the target fixed could not be achieved. What are the factors responsible for unsatisfactory results of development administration in India? The answer is given below.

It is an open fact that the success of any programme of action depends on the public response and participation. In the words of S.N. Misra and K. Sharma, "with a view to forestalling the dangers of bureaucratic elitism and totalitarianism, people's participation becomes imperative." Research studies made in the field of rural development through the Panchayati Raj Institutions in India brings the fact to the light that developments have gone to the economically better-off socially high-ups in social stratification and the politically advantaged sections of rural communities.[23] The studies reveal the fact that the weaker sections have either been deprived of the processes or marginally benefited. It is evident from the statement issued by the Sixth Five Year Plan which stated that "much of the benefits from infrastructure have accured largely to the relatively affluent. Many segments of population like Scheduled Castes and Tribes have not shared fully in benefit growth.[24] The Ashok Mehta Committee on Panchayati Raj Institutions, too, reported that Panchayati Raj Institutions are dominated by economically and socially privileged sections of society and have as such facilitated the emergence of oligarchic forces yielding no benefits to weaker sections."[25]

The social structure of Indian society is such that it is

characterised by numerous divisions along linguistic, ethnic, religious and economic lines. The groups having approach to political elites and maintaining their might in the society, tend to bend the machinery and processes of the Government to their side and thus monopolise the fruit of development administration. They influence the processes by offering bribes to the corrupt Government officials. According to the Santhanam Committee on Prevention of Corruption the discretionary powers exercised by different categories of Government officials opened up "scope for harassment, mal-practices and corruption."[26] Honesty and morality are two great factors which keep the administrative machinery on constant smooth run. Administration is a power and power corrupts the man. Corruption is a common problem of administration. Corruption has become a way of life in India. It prevails from top to bottom of the Indian society. It is corruption which has badly influenced the social, political and economic fabrics of the Indian society. Various Commissions and Committees set up to find out facts about corruption in administration from time to time have proved the fact that corruption prevails in Indian administration from head to toe. It has been discovered that several Ministers as well as high officials are indulged in corruption either for money or for managing benefits for their kin and kith.[27] Bribry is the most prevalent way of corruption in India. A general idea prevails among the general Indian mass that nothing, but bribery can produce the desired results.

Promulgation of new Regulations, need for issue of new licenses and permits due to sudden extension of economic activities after the arrival of development administration, increased the number of administrative processes enlarging the administrative actions. The operational scope of, for instance, the Community Development Project and the National Extension Services has become so vast that officers sitting at all levels may freely exercise a great will of their discretion outside the four walls of law and Regulations. The union of power and discretion vested at different levels in the execution of development scheme is, thus, bound to produce corruption.

The subordinate officers, having got delegated powers, also makes delay in actions knowingly just for receiving bribes from the parties concerned. It has become their habit. Moreover, the administrative powers and growth of discretionary powers opened new ways for harassment to the public, malpractices and corruption among the vested interests.[28] Again, unwillingness of the Government to deal drastically with the corrupt and inefficient public servants is also one of the factors responsible for the growth of corruption in development administration. It has been observed that the corrupt officials, having links with the political leaders, are hardly punished. In fact, generally Heads of Departments are themselves corrupt and a corrupt official can never combat corruption in his Department. As a result, corruption has become a perpetual profession of the Government servants.[29] Declination of moral standard and values in public life has also given strength of corruption. A man without moral standard may neither be afraid or ashamed of his bad and corrupt practices. Even the public as a whole without high standard of morality cannaot check or protest corruption with the result that corruption in India has made deep dent in the soceity.

Despite various steps taken by both the Government of India and State Governments to curb down the rising hydera heads of corruption, corruption is rising day by day. It has been observed that the anti-corruption departments and agencies find themselves embarrassed to deal with the corrupt officials due to undue interference of the political leaders. It has rightly been observed that "No drive against corruption can succeed unless and until the Government itself is firmly committed to the task of weeding out dishonest and corrupt officials, irrespective of rank and status. The punishment for corruption should be exemplary, the least being dismissal from service."[39]

Besides corruption, there are various factors which are working as barriers between the Government officials and the public. Some of such factors are mentioned below:

1. People's ignorance about procedures and processes involved in getting things done;
2. unhelpful attitudes of officials directly concerned with development administration;
3. favouratism and nepotism;
4. need for middlemen to get thing done;
5. Rich-poor discrimination in administration;
6. legancy of colonial attitudes of bureaucracy;
7. Intervention in administrative affairs by Ministers, M.L.As, M.Ps. and public leaders; and
8. intervention by ruling political parties in administrative affairs to help their supporters.

To reach the benefits of development schemes to every family in India there is an emergent need to exercise the political powers in such a manner that not only the organised groups should get the benefits but those who are still unorganised, unaware and neglected should have their share without any further delay. Delay will cause more dissatisfaction, unrest and disappointment among the poor which may take the shape of revolt against the haves by the havenots.

References

1. For detail study of District Administration in India during the British period, see B.B. Misra, District Administration and Rural Development (Delhi, 1983).
2. See the Preamble of the Constitution of India.
3. Nehru's Message Summary Record of Annual Conference on Community Development held at Mount Abu, published by the Ministry of Community Development, Government of India (New Delhi, 1960), p. 13.
4. Fifth-Five Year Plan, Government of India (Delhi, 1952), p. 223.
5. Community Development Panchayati Raj and Cooperative,

Publication Division, Government of India (New Delhi, 1964), p. 6.

6. Evaluation of Report on Second Year Working of Community Project Series No. 27, pp. 2-7.

7. B.B. Misra, Government and Bureaucracy in India, 1947-76, (New Delhi, 1986), p. 352.

8. Ibid., p. 351.

9. Seventh Evaluation Report on Community Development and Allied Fields (New Delhi Programme Evaluation Organisation) Planning Commission, Government of India, 1960, pp. 121-35.

10. Report of the Team for the Study of Community Project, National Extension Services, Vol. I (New Delhi, 1957), p. 5.

11. Ibid., p. 7.

12. Ibid., p. 7.

13. B.B. Misra, District Administration and Rural Development, op. cit., p. 331.

14. Thimmaiah G., District Level Planning in T.K. Lakshman and B.K. Narainan (Eds) Rural Development in India—A multi-dimensional Analysis (Bombay, 1984), pp. 59-60.

15. B.P. Mathai, "Organisation Design for Rural Development in North-East Region", P.D. Sekia and U. Phukan (Eds) (Delhi, 1989), p. 49.

16. G.P. Bhave "Institutional Finance and Integrated Rural Development", Kurukshetra, Vol. XXIX, No. 20, July 16-31, 1981, Bombay, p. 5.

17. Planning Commission, Government of India, Sixth Five Year Plan (1980-85) New Delhi, 1981, p. 32.

18. *Gramin Vikas News Letters*, Vol. I, No. II, Nov. 1985, published by the Department of Rural Development, Ministry of Agriculture, Government of India, Delhi, pp. 2-3.

19. Ibid., Vol. II, No. 2, February, 1986, p. 2.

20. Guidelines of Rural Industries Component of IRDP/TRYSEM, Government of India, 1979, Annexure-I.

21. *Gramin Vikas Newsletters*, Vol. 5, No. 8-9, op. cit., p. 18.

22. Jawahar Rojgar Yojana, a Manual published by Department of Rural Development, Government of India, August, 1989.

23. C. Srinivas Sastry, "Structure and Pattern of Panchayati Raj," *Indian Journal of Public Administration*, Vol. VIII, No. 4, October-December, 1962, p. 460.

24. T.K. Roy, "Some Thoughts on Community Participation," *Kurukshetra*, Vol. XXXI, May 16-31, 1983, p. 18.

25. Samual J. Elders Veld, V. Jangnadham, A.P., The Citizens and the Administrators in Developing Society, (New Delhi, 1968).

26. Report of the Committee on Prevention of Corruption (New Delhi), Ministry of Home Affairs, 1964, para 2 and 16.

27. S.N. Dwivedy, "Corruption in Indian Administration", S.N. Bhale Rao, (Ed) Administration, Politics and Development, Bombay, 1972, p. 220.

28. Srinivas Sastry, "Structure and Pattern of Panchayati Raj", *Indian Journal of Public Administration*, Vol. VIII, No. 4, Oct.-Dec. 1962, p. 460.

29. The Report of Rural-Urban Relationship Committee, New Delhi, Government of India, 1966, pp. 1-10.

30. Hosiar Singh and Mohinder Singh, Public Administration in India, (New Delhi, 1979), p. 209.

Conclusion

Before independence the major goal before the people of India was to achieve freedom and set up the popular Government of their own. When this objective was achieved, the major objective was to liberate the people of India from mass poverty and provide social justice to them. In other words, after the dawn of Independence the problem which very much confronted the Indian leaders was to minimise the social tension and inequality in India which was raising its head due to big gap between the rich and the poor which was the consequence of the British economic policies. The Constitution of India provided enough scope by incorporating socialistic principles to bring about basic change in the socio-economic pattern of the society. Though no work like 'socialism' or 'socialistic pattern of society' was included in the constitution of India, the principles contained in the Fourth Part of the constitution known as Directive Principles of State Policy obviously indicate that the objectives of the constitution makers were to mould the country gradually towards a socialistic pattern of society. The preamble of the constitution, too, which speaks about the aims and objectives of the constitution indicates that the constitution has firm intention to provide social, economic and political justice for the people of India.

The Congress Government which assumed the power and responsibility to implement the principles of justice began to face hard and stiff resistance from the conservative forces when it started to give practical shape to these principles. As a result a tug-of-war took place between the Indian judiciary and the legislature for interpretating the constitution or amending it according to the contemporary conditions and need. Much energy was lost in this regard and there was too much tension between the forces of the progressive and conservative. It killed much time with the result that for several years the principles of social justice could not be implemented with greater speed and satisfactory manner. The constitution was evalauted several times with a view to removing obstacles from the progressive path of the Government. However, the mouth of the Indian judiciary was shut up to a great extent by making bigger surgery (Forty Second Amendment) in the constitution which enabled the Government to go ahead with greater speed. Thereafter, the Government adopted various ways and means to give practical effect to the principles of social justice for general well-being of the poor, backward, weaker and down-trodden sections of people. A decisive push also given to the planned economy of the country by diverting huge amount towards the betterment of the rural poor people living in the country. As a result the very objective of the Sixth and Seventh Five Year Plans of India became to remove poverty from the country by providing more avenues for rural employment and economic assistance to the poor farmers.

The Indian Parliament and the state legislatures passed several Acts with an intention to give justice to the poor. In the Industrial Sector the Government pass some important laws like Factories Act of 1948, Minimum Wages Act of 1948, Employees State Insurance Act, 1948, Plantation Labour Act, 1951, Mines Act, 1952, Employee Provident Fund Benefit Act of 1952, Maternity Benefit Act of 1961, Payment of Bonus Act of 1965, Payment of Gratuity Act of 1972 etc. All these Acts gave much economic relief to the employed workers under the establishment of the Government or Private Sector.

In the Agrarian Sector, too, the Government took up several measures to help the farmers and eradicate poverty. The abolition of Landlordism Act and Land Reforms Acts as well as Land Ceiling Acts were passed all over the country.

The legislatures also passed some welfare Acts. The Government took up several measures to deal with social evils like untouchability and dowry system. The Untouchability Offences Act of 1955 and the Dowry Prohibition Act of 1961 are the examples which certify the steps of the Government taken towards the welfare of the people by stopping wrong social practices. To give special help to the Scheduled Castes and Tribes of India the Government made special provisions for their well being by reserving seats in the educational institutions for admission and in the Government establishment for services. The provisions of protective discrimination has been made and renewed after every tenth year so as to give as special boost to the under privileged sections of the community.

From the very beginning the Planning Commission of India worked with emphasis on providing justice to the poor and weaker sections of the country. The Planning Commission frankly admitted that "In the implementation of the programmes, the weakest are looked after and the benefits of development are made to flow by planned investment in the under-developed regions and among the more backward sections of the community."[1]

With a view to realising the goal of socio-economic justice in the country Mrs. Indira Gandhi launched her new 20-Point Programme on January 14, 1982. These programmes touched some of the most important social and economic issues included in the Sixth Plan and "seek to impart greater dynamism to these. While the thrust of the revised programme continued to be on providing better living conditions for the less privileged sections of the population, it also aims at all-round improvement of productivity."[2] The programmes laid particular stress on items designed to ameliorate the social and economic conditions of the poor and less privileged sections of the community. The strengthening and expansion of the coverage of the integrated rural development and national rural employment programmes, implementation of agricultural land ceilings and distribution of surplus land as well as the growth of the handicrafts, handlooms, small and village industries are intended to increase employment, strengthen the resource base of the rural poor and raise their incomes. Moreover, these programmes proposed to accelerate the development programmes having a bearing on the welfare of the Scheduled Castes, Scheduled Tribes and bonded labourers.

Beside the Government agencies, several voluntary organisations also joined hands with the Government to provide social justice to the poor and deprived sections of the community. The People's Action for Development (India), a nodal organisation for voluntary agencies actively engaged in promoting voluntary efforts. Its aim was to provide financial assistance to voluntary organisations to implement rural development projects, taking the initiative in promoting the voluntary agencies and buildings up local leadership and organising training for voluntary organsiations, rural workers and beneficiaries. The People's Action for Development was set up mainly for canalising funds from foreign sources. It is actively associated with the implementation of the programme of Development of Women and Children in Rural Areas (DWCRA) and Promotion of Voluntary Schemes and Social Action Programme.[3]

It was realised that the Rural Development Department alone would not be enough to meet the new challenges of women's development. Hence in 1984-85 a decision was taken that voluntary organisations would be assisted from Central Source to implement the Development of Women and Children in Rural India. So it was decided to provide assistance to voluntary agencies through the People's Action Department. This Department organised several conferences of leading voluntary organisations to disseminate the programme, generate project proposals and decide modalities of implementing the scheme of assistance to the voluntary agencies. Thus it is obvious that several programmes and schemes were adopted all over the country and several agencies were involved to implement these programmes and schemes with only intention to remove poverty and provide economic relief to the people belonging to the poor and weaker sections of the society.

So far the district of Nalanda is concerned, as a small administrative unit of the state, like other districts it also received instructions and funds to give effect to those schemes and programmes. The agencies of the Government applied efforts to make a success in this regard. The district authorities spent huge amount of money which it received through several agencies and the Five Year Plans. No scheme was left untouched.

But it should be noted that no marked change occurred in the living standard of people or poverty has been removed either from Nalanda district or from any part of the country. A thorough investigation into the implementation of the adopted Government's policies and programmes in this regard reflects a very sad disappointing and discouraging picture. Nearly four decades of independence of the country have passed, but no satisfactory improvement has been made in the life of those people who belonged to the weaker and poor sections. On the other hand, the vast majority of people are shrouded in and sunk into acute poverty facing a number of difficulties. Their economic conditions are worsening day by day. Their dirty economic condition and insecured dark and gloomy future have not only caused worries to them but also dampened their spirit. They are disappointed, unsatisfied and irritiated. They are still deprived of the due benefits of the welfare and social schemes. On the other hand, a handful of persons belonging to the upper stratum of the society are the best beneficiaries of these welfare and social schemes. By nature they are selfish, greedy, cunning, shrewd and demagogic. Their only aim of life is to accumulate as much property as they can even at the cost of Nation's safety and security. Luxuries and comforts are these two basic criteria to judge the value of human life according to the rich sections of the Indian people. For the achievement of luxuries and comforts they may go down to any extent. They may involve into dirty politics, social clashes, bloodshed and murder even.

There are various reasons behind the failure of the Government of Bihar and authorities of Nalanda to successfully implement the ways and measures which stood for removing poverty and economic inequalities from the society. But the most important reason is the lack of commitment of the Government to its policies and programmes and mass corruption prevailed among the Government servants from top to bottom. That is why the benefits of these programmes did to got to the required sections of the society. According to V.M. Dandekar and Nilkanth Rath, the benefits of development have been shared among the affluent sections of the Indian society. The Mahalanobis Committee which was appointed by the Planning Commission in 1960 with a view to finding out how the incomes generated during the first two Plans were distributed in the country, reported that "despite all countervailing measures, the concentration of economic power in the private sector is more than which could be justified." According to the Planning Commission, too, "the percentage of population below the poverty line in 1977-78 may be projected at 48% in rural areas and 41% in urban areas. The total number of the poor, so defined would be about 270 million. About 160 million of them fall below 7% of the poverty lines."[4]

Thus it is quite clear that there is extreme inequalities in income and wealth in India. The reports submitted by various committees and commissions which studies the progress of the Indian Plans and programmes concluded the same truth. They all agreed that so far the distribution of the national income is concerned, it is the common factor that a substantial number of people are living under the poverty line facing a number of difficulties and inconveniences.[5] No doubt the national income went on increasing under each plan, but the problem of economic inequality remained as it was.

The practice of mixed economy in India also provided ample opportunities to the rich sections of India to accumulate huge amount of property and national wealth. A.K. Wagchi rightly maintained that the government of the mixed economies are extremely inhibited about curtailing the right to private property fundamentally and the alternative controlling mechanism, it tries to set up, comes ultimately to be governed by the more dominant forces in the economic, viz. the expenditure pattern of the Private Sector."[6] In India despite several regulations the Private Sector gradually came prominance developing its hold on the production of unnecessary luxury goods and earned huge amount of money. On the other hand, the Government was forced to function through a variety of fiscal, monetary and physical controls with the result that it caused several administrative problems. This also encouraged black-money, red tappism, corruption etc.

Several schemes like Cooperative Farmings, Joint Cooperative Farmings, Community Development Programme, Integrated Rural Development Programme, Rural Landless Employment Guarantee Programme etc. failed to achieve the required results due to non-commitment of the Government and mass corruption prevailed among the Government servants. In the case of Nalanda District it is surprising to note that the Block Development Officers and their associated staff whose real assignment is to help the farmers and the poor persons in getting the benefits of the several Rural Development Schemes, are least interested in their jobs. Instead of helping them these officers and government personnels along with Pradhans, Mukhias, Surpanch, Pramukhs, Gram Sevaks, Village Level Workers etc. are busy with usurping the major or whole portion of the Government's financial aids provided for the development of the rural areas. The basic assignment of the Village Level Workers and the Gram Sevaks are to assist the farmers and other concerned people, but they rarely do their jobs. Consequently, the poor, backward and illiterate village cultivators and workers remained deprived of their share of the national income and other benefits.

Despite various steps taken by the Government to remove unemployment from the district of Nalanda, the unemployment is mounting over. These unemployed youths and jobless workers, being conscious of their rights are organising themselves on the line of class-antagonism and class-war. They have lost their faith in the principles of social justice incorporated in the constitution. They have also lost their faith in the ways and means adopted by the Government to remove poverty and reduce economic inequality. In the words of Chandrika Singh "the prevailing unpleasant and unfavourable circumstance will not take much time to send them (dissatisfied poor workers) to front line of politics with the aim to assert and fight for their rights."[7]

It cannot be denied that the deprived and unprivileged sections of the community have got some relief from the economic policies of the Government. However, but it is also a fact that no marked changes have appeared in the day-do-day life of those people who are living at the bottom of the social stratum. It is all because widely prevalence of nepotism, favouritism and corruption blocked the way of progess of the general mass. The administrative machinery of the Government of Nalanda district is so loose, inactive and corrupt that it is beyond its capacity to give justice to the required sections. Even some corrupt Ministers, Members of Parliament, Members of Legislative Assembly are also found joining hands with the corrupt people. In fact, it were those persons who encouraged the practice of nepotism, favouritism and corruption in the society of Nalanda. The Government servants are found indulged into open bribery system. Bribery is very common in Nalanda and it has become common affairs in day-to-day life of public administration. As a result those who have approach to higher authorities or have enough money to bribe them are able to receive the maximum benefit of the running welfare schemes in Nalanda district.

History witnesses the fact that huge amount of blood has been shed on the earth to recognise and establish human status on the basis of equality and social justice. Unless firm decision is taken establish justice and its opponents are suppressed mercilessly, justice cannot be established and practiced. So far the case of India is concerned, it requires firm determination and commitment to provide justice to the weaker and deprived sections of the society. No doubt, the people of India is far better in comparison to the period of the British Raj. But it is not enough. To make India a society of socialistic matter a lot has to be done.

To discipline the Government servants upon whose shoulders the responsibility to implement the policies lies, there is an urgent need to take very strict disciplinary action against those who are found indulged in corruption or those who are shirking from the responsibility. It is observed that the bureaucratic pattern of India is still based on the line established by the British whose only aim was to maintain law and order, and collect revenues. Since Independent India is committed to a welfare state, the Indian bureaucrats should be compelled to change their old concept of thinking. They should realise that they are servants of the people not the masters. To corrupt authorities must be given hard punishment including discharge from their services. It would be better if some special courts are constituted with the power to award summary decision to deal with such corrupt administrators or Government servants. A liquidation drive against the corrupt Government servants must be launched without any further delay.

Secondly to make the society free from the antisocial elements like smugglers, hoarders, black markeeters, rumour mongers etc. suitable laws with severe penalty must be passed. No mercy should be shown to these elements because they are the real enemy of the people and nation both. These elements are parasite which grow up at the cost of the poor and backward sections of the society.

Thirdly, special drive should be launched to unearth black money. It is a fact that the Government has failed to arrest tax evasion and unearth blackmoney. The public works have been badly affected due to stagnation of money. Hence all the possible efforts should be applied in this regard. Moreover, some changes should be brought in the system of taxation so that more money should be collected from the wealthy persons. The system of inherited right is unsuitable in India keeping in view the prevailed mass poverty. Therefore it must be abolished.

Fourthly, efforts must be applied to increase the essential commodities and foodgrains by giving incentives to the best farmers and producers. The system of irrigation should be improved and it should be ensured that whether the farmers are getting continuous electric supply for cultivation or not.

References

1. Planning Commission of India (New Delhi), *Fourth-Five Year Plan* (1969), p. 28.

2. *India: A Reference Annual*, 1982, pp. 209-10.

3. See, *Gramin Vikas Newsletter*, Vol. 1, No. 11, November, 1985, published by Department of Rural Development, Ministry of Agriculture, New Delhi, p. 1.

4. Government of India, Planning Commission, *Draft Five Year Plan*, 1978-83, (New Delhi, 1978), p. 3.

5. Government of India, Planning Commission, Sixth-Five Year Plan, 1980-85, Annexure 1, 12, p. 16.

6. A.K. Wagchi, "Long-Term Constraint of India's Industrial Growth, 1951-1966", E.A.G. Robinson and Michel Kidron (Eds.), *Economic Development in South Asia*, (London, 1970), p. 172.

7. Chandrika Singh, *Socialism in India* (New Delhi, 1986), p. 206.

Bibliography

Primary Sources

Constituent Assembly Debates, 1946, 1947 and 1948, Government of India, New Delhi.

Speeches of Pt. Jawaharlal Nehru, Vol. I and II (1935-57) Ministry of Publication and Broadcasting, Government of India, New Delhi, 1958 and 1962.

India Quarterly Register II, 1929, New Delhi.

Indian Annual Register, 1934, New Delhi.

Indian Annual Register, Vol. II, 1936, New Delhi.

Constitution of India, Ministry of Law, Justice and Company Affairs, Government of India, New Delhi, 1980.

Constitution of India, Allahabad Law Agency, Allahabad, 1965. Census of India 1951, Vol. VI.

First Five Year Plan, Planning Commission, Government of India, New Delhi.

Second Five Year Plan, Planning Commission, Government of India, New Delhi.

Third Five Year Plan, Planning Commission, Government of India, New Delhi.

Fourth Five Year Plan, Planning Commission, Government of India, New Delhi.

Fifth Five Year Plan, Planning Commission, Government of India, New Delhi.

Sixth Five Year Plan, Planning Commission, Government of India, New Delhi.

Seventh Five Year Plan, Planning Commission, Government of India, New Delhi.

Eighth Five Year Plan, Planning Commission, Government of India, New Delhi.

Secondary Sources

(A) Books

Acharaya, Balaswami, *A Struggle for Freedom*, Delhi, 1958.

Adhikari, S., *Communist Party and India's Path to National Regeneration and Socialism*, New Delhi, 1964.

Agrawal, R.C., *Indian Constitutional Development and National Movement*, New Delhi, 1956.

Ali, Sadiq, *Indian National Congress: Resolution on Economic Policy Programme and Allied Matters*, 1924-1968, New Delhi.

Ali, Sadiq, *Towards Socialist Thinking in Congress*, New Delhi, 1960.

A.M. & Zaidi, S.C., *Encyclopedia of the Indian National Congress*, Vol. I, II, III, IV, V, VI, VII, VIII, IX and X, New Delhi.

Azad, Abul Kalam, *India Wins Freedom*, Bombay, 1969.

Bailey, F.G., *Politics and Social Changes in India*, Orissa, 1959.

Bandyopadhayay, J., *The Congress and Socialism*, New Delhi, 1968.

Banerjee, M., *Planning in India*, New Delhi, 1968.

Besant, Annie, *How India Wrought for Freedom*, (*The Story of the Indian National Congress*), New Delhi, 1975.

Banerjee, S.C. *Indian Constitutional Documents* (Three Volumes), Calcutta, 1948-49.

Bhashin, Prem, *Congress and Socialism*, New Delhi, 1963.

Betelle Andre, *Castes: Old and New Essays in Social Structure and Social Stratification*, Bombay, 1969.

Brecher, Michael, *Succession in India: A Study in Decision Making*, London, 1966.

Brecher, Michael, *Nehru: A Political Biography*, Oxford, 1959.

Basu, D.D., *Introduction to Constitution of India*, New Delhi, 1978.

Basu, D.D., *Constitutional Law of India*, New Delhi, 1977.

Caveesher, S.S., *India's Fight for Freedom: A Critical Study of the Indian National Movement since the Advent of Mahatma Gandhi in the Field of Indian Politics*, Lahore, 1936.

Chand Tara, *History of the Freedom Movement in India*, Vol. I, New Delhi.

Chand Tara, *History of Freedom Movement in India*, Vol. II, New Delhi.

Chand Tara, *History of Freedom Movement in India*, Vol. III, New Delhi.

Chandra Bipin, *Rise and Growth of Economic Nationalism in India*, Delhi, 1967.

Choudhary, S., *Peasants' and Workers' Movements in India*, 1905, 1929, New Delhi, 1971.

Charles, Bettleheim, *India Independent*, 1971.

Cocker, F.W., *Recent Political Thought*, Calcutta, 1971.

Colebrook, H.T., *Remarks of Husbandry in Bengal*, Sidney Lee, 1906.

Cole, G.D.H. *Socialism in Evolution*, London, 1938.

Cole, G.D.H., *The Simple Case of Socialism*, London, 1935.

Croker, Water, *Nehru: A Contemporary Estimate*, London, 1967.

Dandekar, V.M. and Nilkantha Rath, *Poverty in India*, Bombay, 1971.

Daniel, Thorney, *The Agrarian, Prospects in India*, Delhi, 1976.

Desai, A.R., *Social Background and Indian Socialism*, Bombay, 1966.

Dev, Narendra, *Socialism and National Revolution*, Bombay, 1956.

Dev, Narendra, *Samajvad Ka Muladhar*, Banaras, 1949.

Dewet, K.R. and Verma, J.D., *Indian Economy*, New Delhi, 1948.

Dikshit, C., *Democratic Socialism in India*, New Delhi, 1971.

Druhe, David M., *Soviet Russia and Indian Communism*, New York, 1959.

Earnest Barker, *Political Thought in England - 1948-1915*, London, 1915.

Ebenstin, W., *Modern Political Thought*, (2nd edition), New Delhi, 1970.

Ebenstin, W., *Great Political Thinker*, Calcutta, 1972.

Edward, M., *The Last Year of British Rule*, London, 1963.

Engles, F., *Socialism Utopia and Scientific*, London, 1892.

Eradman, Howord L., *The Swatantra Party and Indian Conservatism*, Cambridge, 1967.

Franda Marcus, F., *Radical Politics in West Bengal*, London, 1971.

Gadgil, A.R., *Origin of the Modern Indian Business Class*, New York, 1959.

Ganguli, C., *Studies in Indian Economic Problems*, New Delhi, 1980.

Ganguli, B.N. and Gupta, B.B., *Level of Livings in India*, New Delhi, 1976.

Gregg Richiard, B., *Which way Lies Hope? An Examination of Capitalism, Socialism and Gandhi's Programmes*, Allahabad, 1957.

Griffths, Percival, *British Impact on India*, London, 1952.

Ghosh, P.C., *Indian National Congress - 1892-1900*, Calcutta, 1960.

Hollingberry, *Zamindari Settlement of Bengal*, Vol. I, Calcutta, 1979.

Iyangar, K.B., Sriniwasa, *Sri Aurobindo*, Calcutta, 1950.

Jennings Ivor, *Some Characteristics of Indian Constitution*, London, 1953.

Karnik, V.B., *Indian Trade Union*, Bombay, 1960.

Kaushik, P.D., *The Congress Ideology and Programmes*, 1920-1947, Bombay, 1964.

Keith, AB., *Speeches and Documents on Indian Policy*, London,1922.

Keker, S.V., *History of Caste in India*, Jaipur, 1979.

Kriplani, J.B., *Gandhi, His Life and Thought*, New Delhi, 1964.

Kochack, Stanley, A., *The Congress Party of India: The Dynamics of One Party Democracy*, Princeton, 1980.

Kumar Shive, *Peasantry and Indian National Movement*, 1919-1933.

Laski, H.J., *Communism, 1881-1927*, London, 1927.

Lal, H.B., *Congress Brand of Socialism: A Critical Review*, Varanasi, 1964.

Lohia, R.M., *Aspects of Socialist Policy*, Bombay, 1955.

Madhok Balraj, *Political Trends in India*, Delhi, 1959.

Masani, Minoo, *The Congress Path to Communism*, Bombay, 1961.

Marx, Karl & Fredrick Engeles, *Manifesto of Communist* Party, Moscow, 1977.

Masani, Minoo, *The Communist Party of India*, A Short History, Bombay, 1967.

Mandelbaum, W., *Prospects for Indian Development*, London, 1962.

Mazumdar, B., *History of Indian Social and Political Ideas*, Calcutta, 1967.

Mehta, Ashok, *The Political Mind of India*, Bombay, 1952.

Misra, B.B., *The Indian Middle Class*, London, 1961.

Misra, B.B., *The Indian Political Parties* (2nd edition), New Delhi, 1978.

Mishra, O.P., *Economic Policy of Pt. Jawaharlal Nehru*, Allahabad, 1968.

Mishra, D.P., *Living an Era*: Nehru, Vol. II, New Delhi, 1978.

Mishra, S.K. and Puri, V.K., *Indian Economy*, Delhi, 1983.

Minhas, B.S., *Planning and the Poor*, New Delhi, 1974.

Moris Jones, W.H., *The Government and Politics of India*, Bombay, 1952.

Namboodiripad, E.M.S., *India Under Congress*, Calcutta, 1964.

Narayan, J.P., *From Socialism to Sarvodaya*, Kashi, 1957.

Narayan, J.P., *Towards Struggle*, Bombay, 1946.

Narain, Sriman, *Socialism in Indian Planning*, Delhi, 1964.

Nayar, Kuldip, *The Judgement*, Delhi.

Nehru, J., *Towards Freedom*, New Delhi, 1955.

Nehru, J., *India and the World*, London, 1935.

Nehru, J., *Towards Freedom*, New Delhi, 1955.

Nehru, J., *Autobiography*, Bombay, 1962.

Nehru, J., *A Bunch of Old Letters*, Bombay, 1960.

Rao, M.S., (ed) *Social Movement in India*, Vol. I, II, and III Delhi, 1978.

Raman, Pattabhi, N., *Political Involvement of Indian Trade Unions*, London, 1967.

Rasual, A.A., *History of the All India Kisan Sabha*, 1974.

Roosevelt, E., *India and Awakening of East.*

Roy, R., "Masses in Indian Politics," *Economic and Social History Review*, Delhi, 1974.

Rosen, Jorge, *Discovery and Economic Change in India*, Bombay, 1966.

Roy, M.N., *India in Transition*, Genewa, 1922.

Roy, M.N., *The Future of Indian Politics*, 1971.

Roy, S., *Indian Politics and Constitutional Development*, Meerut, 1976.

Sarain, L.N., *J. Nehru*, Delhi, 1963.

Sen, Shusil, *Peasants Movements in India*, Delhi, 1982.

Seal, A., *Emergency of Indian Socialism: Competition and Collaboration in later Nineteenth Century*, Cambridge, 1964.

Sriniwas, Y. Thakur, *Indian Economic Development*, New Delhi, 1982.

Shills Edward, *The Intellectuals Between Transition and Modernity, The Indian Situation*, Hague, 1961.

Sharma, J.S., *J. Nehru: A Descriptive Biography*, New Delhi, 1955.

Sharma, B.G., *The Political Philosophy of M.N. Roy*, Delhi, 1965.

Singh Chandrika, *Socialism in India: Rise, Growth and Prospects*, New Delhi, 1986.

Singh Raghubir, *Social Change in Indian Society*, Delhi, 1977.

Singh, L.D., *The Left Wing in India*, Muzaffarpur, 1965.

Sriniwarna and Vardhan, P.R., (ed.) *Poverty and Income Distribution in India*, Calcutta, 1974.

Sitaramaya Pattabhi, B., *History of the Indian National Congress*, 2 Vols., Delhi, 1969.

Suda, J.P., *Social and Political Thought in India*, Vols. I, II, and III, Meerut, 1973.

Susobhan Chandra Sanker, (ed) *Ram Mohan Roy on Indian Economy* compiled on behalf of Socio-Economic Research Institute, Calcutta, 1965.

Tendulker, D.G., *Mahatma Gandhi: Collection of His Writings and Speeches*, 8 Vols., Publication Division, Government of India, Delhi, 1960-63.

Thorner Daniel, *The Agrarian Prospects in India*, Delhi, 1976.

Tripathi, A., *The Extremist Challenge*, New Delhi, 1967.

Winner Myron, *State Politics in India*, Princeton, 1968.

Zaid, A.M., *The Annual Register of Indian Political Parties*, New Delhi, 1981.

Zinkin, Taya, *Caste Today*, London, 1962.

Zocharies, H.C.E., *Renaissance in India: From Ram Mohan Roy to Mohandas Gandhi*, London, 1933.

Articles

Moris, Cinsberg, "Special Change," *British Journal of Sociology*, Vol. IX, Calcutta, 1958.

Joshi, P.C., "Land Reforms Implementation and Role of Administrators," *Economic and Political Weekly*, September, 1968.

Gladgil, A., "Changing Views in Developing Countries," *The Swaraj Weekly*, 20.6.1964, Madras.

Lydall, F.H., "The Inequalities of Indian Economies," *Weekly*, Special Number, June, 1960.

Ojha, P.D., and Bhatt V.V., "Pattern of Income Distribution in India, 1953-54 to 1963-65", *Poverty and Income Distribution in India*, Calcutta, 1974.

Bagchi, A.K., "Long Term Contribution of India's Industrial Growth, 1951-1966", in Robinson and M. Kadron (eds) *Economic Development in South Asia*, London, 1970.

Reports Notes and Bulletins

Report of the Task Force on Agrarian Problems, New Delhi.

Report of N.C.A.E.R. Urban Income and Saving, New Delhi, 1962.

Report of the Indian National Congress, Karachi Session, 1931.

Report of the Mahalanobis Committee on Distribution of Income and Level of Livings, Delhi, 1964.

Report of the R.B.I. on Distribution of Income in the Indian Economy: 1953-54 to 1962, *R.B.I. Bulletin*, September, 1962.

Report of the I.N.C., 37th Session at Gaya.

Report of the I.N.C., 47th Session, 1929, at Lahore.

Report of the I.N.C., 1936, 49th Session at Allahabad.

N.C.A.R.E. *All India Consumer Expenditure Survey*, Vol. I and II, New Delhi, 1966-67.

Newspapers, Journals, Magazines, Weekly etc.

British Journal of Sociology, Calcutta.

Kessing Contemporary Archives, London.

Asian Recorders, New Delhi.

Economic and Political Weekly, Delhi.

The Swaraj Weekly.

The Asiatic Quarterly Review, London.

The Modern Review, Calcutta.

The Illustrated Weekly of India, Delhi.

The Hindustan Times, New Delhi.

The Tribune, Chandigarh.

The Statesman, Calcutta.

The Harijan, Ahmedabad.

India Today, New Delhi.

Index

O

P

R

W

Z

□□□